INTRODUCING
ISSUES WITH
OPPOSING
VIEWPOINTS®

Capitalism and Moral Responsibility

Lisa Idzikowski, Book Editor

GREENHAVEN
PUBLISHING

TEEN
174
Capitalism

Published in 2020 by Greenhaven Publishing, LLC
353 3rd Avenue, Suite 255, New York, NY 10010

First Edition

Articles in Greenhaven Publishing anthologies are often edited for length to meet page requirements. In addition, original titles of these works are changed to clearly present the main thesis and to explicitly indicate the author's opinion. Every effort is made to ensure that Greenhaven Publishing accurately reflects the original intent of the authors. Every effort has been made to trace the owners of the copyrighted material.

Library of Congress Cataloging-in-Publication Data

Names: Idzikowski, Lisa, editor.
Title: Capitalism and moral responsibility / Lisa Idzikowski, book editor.
Description: First edition. | New York : Greenhaven Publishing, 2020. |
  Series: Introducing issues with opposing viewpoints | Includes
  bibliographical references and index. | Audience: Grades 7-12.
Identifiers: LCCN 2018056915| ISBN 9781534505766 (library bound) | ISBN
  9781534505773 (pbk.)
Subjects: LCSH: Capitalism—Moral and ethical aspects.
Classification: LCC HB501 .C2423425 2020 | DDC 174/.4—dc23
LC record available at https://lccn.loc.gov/2018056915

Manufactured in the United States of America

Website: http://greenhavenpublishing.com

Contents

Chapter 3: How Should a Capitalistic Society Change for the Better?

Foreword

I ndulging in a wide spectrum of ideas, beliefs, and perspectives is a critical cornerstone of democracy. After all, it is often debates over differences of opinion, such as whether to legalize abortion, how to treat prisoners, or when to enact the death penalty, that shape our society and drive it forward. Such diversity of thought is frequently regarded as the hallmark of a healthy and civilized culture. As the Reverend Clifford Schutjer of the First Congregational Church in Mansfield, Ohio, declared in a 2001 sermon, "Surrounding oneself with only like-minded people, restricting what we listen to or read only to what we find agreeable is irresponsible. Refusing to entertain doubts once we make up our minds is a subtle but deadly form of arrogance." With this advice in mind, Introducing Issues with Opposing Viewpoints books aim to open readers' minds to the critically divergent views that comprise our world's most important debates.

Introducing Issues with Opposing Viewpoints simplifies for students the enormous and often overwhelming mass of material now available via print and electronic media. Collected in every volume is an array of opinions that captures the essence of a particular controversy or topic. Introducing Issues with Opposing Viewpoints books embody the spirit of nineteenth-century journalist Charles A. Dana's axiom: "Fight for your opinions, but do not believe that they contain the whole truth, or the only truth." Absorbing such contrasting opinions teaches students to analyze the strength of an argument and compare it to its opposition. From this process readers can inform and strengthen their own opinions, or be exposed to new information that will change their minds. Introducing Issues with Opposing Viewpoints is a mosaic of different voices. The authors are statesmen, pundits, academics, journalists, corporations, and ordinary people who have felt compelled to share their experiences and ideas in a public forum. Their words have been collected from newspapers, journals, books, speeches, interviews, and the Internet, the fastest growing body of opinionated material in the world.

Introducing Issues with Opposing Viewpoints shares many of the well-known features of its critically acclaimed parent series, Opposing

Viewpoints. The articles allow readers to absorb and compare divergent perspectives. Active reading questions preface each viewpoint, requiring the student to approach the material thoughtfully and carefully. Photographs, charts, and graphs supplement each article. A thorough introduction provides readers with crucial background on an issue. An annotated bibliography points the reader toward articles, books, and websites that contain additional information on the topic. An appendix of organizations to contact contains a wide variety of charities, nonprofit organizations, political groups, and private enterprises that each hold a position on the issue at hand. Finally, a comprehensive index allows readers to locate content quickly and efficiently.

Introducing Issues with Opposing Viewpoints is also significantly different from Opposing Viewpoints. As the series title implies, its presentation will help introduce students to the concept of opposing viewpoints and learn to use this material to aid in critical writing and debate. The series' four-color, accessible format makes the books attractive and inviting to readers of all levels. In addition, each viewpoint has been carefully edited to maximize a reader's understanding of the content. Short but thorough viewpoints capture the essence of an argument. A substantial, thought-provoking essay question placed at the end of each viewpoint asks the student to further investigate the issues raised in the viewpoint, compare and contrast two authors' arguments, or consider how one might go about forming an opinion on the topic at hand. Each viewpoint contains sidebars that include at-a-glance information and handy statistics. A Facts About section located in the back of the book further supplies students with relevant facts and figures.

Following in the tradition of the Opposing Viewpoints series, Greenhaven Publishing continues to provide readers with invaluable exposure to the controversial issues that shape our world. As John Stuart Mill once wrote: "The only way in which a human being can make some approach to knowing the whole of a subject is by hearing what can be said about it by persons of every variety of opinion and studying all modes in which it can be looked at by every character of mind. No wise man ever acquired his wisdom in any mode but this." It is to this principle that Introducing Issues with Opposing Viewpoints books are dedicated.

Introduction

"The great dynamic success of capitalism had given us a powerful weapon in our battle against Communism—money.
                        —Ronald Reagan, 40th President of the US

"Capitalism has worked very well. Anyone who wants to move to North Korea is welcome.
                                —Bill Gates, October 2010

"Today everything comes under the laws of competition and the survival of the fittest, where the powerful feed upon the powerless. As a consequence, masses of people find themselves excluded and marginalized; without work, without possibilities, without any means of escape."
                                —Pope Francis, 2013

Capitalism as defined by *Merriam-Webster*, is "a way of organizing an economy so that the things that are used to make and transport products (such as land, oil, factories, ships, etc.) are owned by individual people and companies rather than by the government." It is an important definition because, "Capitalism characterizes the behavior of the global economy. Since the disintegration of the Soviet Union, capitalism has become the dominant economic system worldwide."

Another important issue is the concept of moral responsibility. Many philosophers say that to be morally responsible, an individual usually performs some kind of action, which causes this same person to get some sort of reaction—blame, praise, exultation, or condemnation—depending on the way the individual performed the action. Take an everyday situation. A pedestrian notices a nearby building has caught on fire. Most likely this person would immediately reach for his or her cell phone and dial 911 to report the fire. Most likely the person would be praised for lending a hand to help the situation, and it could be said he or she acted in a morally responsible way. On the other hand, this same pedestrian might walk right past the burning building, not call 911, and instead "mind their own business" or ignore the probable negative situation. And most likely the individual would be labelled as having acted in a morally irresponsible way.

It is interesting to think of an economic system, and at the same time to consider the concept of moral responsibility. Throughout history three economic systems have dominated human culture: capitalism, socialism, and communism. Capitalism is often characterized by the free market economy. It is an economic system where innovation and individualism play a large part. Businesses are owned as private property, aim to make profits, and are run by individuals that are often called capitalists. Socialism and communism are the other two economic systems. They are viewed as being opposites to capitalism in large part because typically their economies and businesses function under tight government control instead of the freedom coming from private ownership. Socialist and communist governments want to control their societies and stamp out individualism. Socialists and communists envision a society or world where people are equal, and all have the same things. They accuse capitalism of resulting in a wealth gap, among other things.

Can capitalism be a moral economic system, and can capitalists function as morally responsible individuals? This simple question on the face of it actually poses a complex issue with experts weighing in on both sides. Greed, and perhaps the image of Gordon Gekko from the movie *Wall Street* and his infamous quote, "Greed, for lack of a better word, is good" is often seen as an evil of the capitalist system. Greed is viewed as a negative behavior by many people, and characters that chase money at all costs and the problems they endure are often portrayed as villains in stories and movies. Opponents of capitalism are no exception to this general thought. They cite an increasing amount of inequality especially in wages, health care, and education as negative consequences of the greed of capitalism and point out that differences in income have been escalating. According to Pew Research, by 2016, the income of middle-class households had not really changed since 2000. Lower class household income had decreased, but the incomes of upper-income households had increased to almost $190,000. Not surprisingly a large portion of

America sees this as unjust. A 2016 Harvard University poll shows that 51 percent of US individuals aged 18 to 29 reject capitalism, while 33 percent favor socialism.

Contrary to this way of thinking are the committed believers of capitalism and its free market system. Proponents of capitalism argue that the system has done a tremendous service to society, and in turn many people around the world have benefitted. They contend that capitalism encourages innovation, and because of it many time-saving and life-saving products such as new technology and medical treatments have been produced throughout history. Think about it—at one time washing clothes was a back-breaking job done by hand, until washing machines were invented and made life easier. As an icon of the technology field Bill Gates embraces capitalism, as do various pharmaceutical companies producing the newest life-saving and life-enhancing medicines.

Do the producers or businesses profit? Sure, they do, but so do consumers. In 1776 Adam Smith penned his classic book, *The Wealth of Nations*, often cited as the basic reference of modern economics. In it Smith writes about a butcher or baker, which are common occupations or businesses of the time period. Smith points out that these business people produced products and sold them to others in exchange for money. He contends that this exchange benefitted both groups, butchers and bakers received money and buyers had meat and bread to feed themselves and their families. These exchanges were voluntary, not overseen by governments, and occurred because of self-interest not greed.

Throughout history and recently, ideas have popped up demanding that changes be made to the free market system. Suggestions have been floated by politicians, business owners, and ordinary citizens. At the Democratic National Convention in 2016 Senator Bernie Sanders called for change and pounded home his idea that it was "not moral, it is not acceptable, and it is not sustainable that the top one-tenth of 1 percent now owns almost as much wealth as the bottom 90 percent." In 2011, citizens marched in the movement dubbed Occupy Wall Street, which attempted to highlight what they believed was wrong in the United States: that the finance industry and corporations had a strangle hold on ordinary people, and inequality was blossoming. Others believe there is nothing inherently wrong with capitalism rather that it is not allowed to function as it should. Steve Forbes, editor-in-chief of *Forbes* magazine and media group (an organization favoring business and capitalism), has written that people don't "have a clear understanding of just what constitutes a 'free' market." He argues that government should "create a stable, hospitable environment for economic activities" and that it's time to admit that "democratic capitalism is the world's greatest success story. No other system has improved the lives of so many people."

One thing is for certain: Debate surrounding the issues related to capitalism and moral responsibility will continue. The diverse viewpoints in *Introducing Issues with Opposing Viewpoints: Capitalism and Moral Responsibility* examine this divisive and ongoing contemporary issue.

Chapter 1

Is Capitalism a Just or Moral System?

The Financial District's Charging Bull statue is a monument to capitalism.

Many People Don't Understand What Capitalism Is

Richard M. Ebeling

"The capitalist system ... leaves everyone free as an individual to live his own life."

In the following excerpted viewpoint Richard M. Ebeling argues that capitalism is misunderstood and used in the wrong contexts. The author seeks to clear up these misconceptions by explaining pure capitalism and providing hypothetical examples of its superiority. Ebeling is the BB&T Distinguished Professor of Ethics and Free Enterprise Leadership at The Citadel, in Charleston, South Carolina.

AS YOU READ, CONSIDER THE FOLLOWING QUESTIONS:

1. What did Karl Marx believe about capitalism according to the viewpoint?
2. What are those who fail to act with respect and courtesy faced with?
3. How is capitalism lined with liberty according to the author?

One of the leading ideological punching bags for well over one hundred years has been the ideas, institutions, and impact of "capitalism" on society. [...] Its most popularized use, no doubt, arose from the writings of Karl Marx and other socialists who were certain that if not for private property in the physical means of production, all of the evils and hardships of humanity could be lifted from mankind's shoulders. Common or "collective" ownership and use of the means of production would soon eliminate poverty, abolish disparities in income and wealth, and bring about a near-post-scarcity world in which "social class" conflicts over possessing things would become a thing of the past.

In the second half of the Twentieth Century, however, the existing socialist "experiments" with collective ownership and government central planning increasingly showed that all they created were political tyrannies, new "status" societies of privilege based on "Party" membership or position within the bureaucracy, and general economic stagnation with standards of living far behind those in "capitalist" countries.

So especially in "the West," those who had been advocates or apologists for, first, the Soviet regime in Russia and then other communist governments around the world, changed their tune. Private property did not have to be abolished outright and in every corner of society. Private enterprise could continue to "deliver the goods," but it needed to be constrained and controlled by a spider's web of regulations and restrictions to see that "capitalism" produced what and where it would best serve the "common good," rather than the directions into which private businessmen would take it guided only by the "profit motive."

The interventionist state had to be accompanied, at the same time, by the welfare state to assure a less "exploitive" and more egalitarian redistribution of wealth through the use of the tax system to take from the "unfairly" richer "Peters" to give to lower income and more deserving "Pauls" in society.

In criticizing the market economy, a common tendency has been to reify "capitalism" as if it were a living, breathing entity acting on and against society. Hence, "Capitalism" exploits the workers.

Those who decry capitalism for exploiting workers might be reluctant to forgo their inexpensive and readily availailable sneakers.

"Capitalism" creates poverty. "Capitalism" destroys the environment. "Capitalism" is "racist." "Capitalism" discriminates against women.

The word has so many negative connotations in so many people's minds that some friends of freedom have suggested to stop using the word at all in designating the economic system that proponents of free enterprise defend; or to add a softer descriptive word to its use. [...]

Private Property, Personal Liberty, and the Polite Society

The bedrock concept behind an explanation of "capitalism" is private property. That is, the idea that an individual has a right of ownership and exclusive use of something. For the classical liberal, the most fundamental property right possessed by an individual is his own person. In other words, an individual owns himself. He may not legally or informally be treated as the slave of another person. The individual has ownership over his mind and his body. Neither may be controlled or commanded by another through the use of force or its threat.

This implies that if every human being has such a right of private ownership over himself, then all associations and relationships between individual human beings must be based upon voluntary consent and mutual agreement. No person may be forced or defrauded into an exchange, trade, or associative relationship.

The classical liberal also believes that if this principle is followed by the community, it tends to create a social setting in which respect and tolerance of others and their choices is more likely to be fostered. Thus, it generates, in various ways, a more humane society. People have the need for each other's assistance and companionship in sundry ways. If force may not be used and only free consent can serve as the basis of those connections among human beings, then it behooves individuals to act with courtesy, deference, and implied dignity toward others.

This does not mean that rude, disrespectful, and even cruel words and deeds may not happen among people. But it does mean that there are costs to doing so since those treated in this manner are less likely to willingly enter into exchanges or other types of relationships with those who treat them in these negative ways. Some might not care and proceed to act in these disrespectful and intolerant ways, anyway. But for most people, the benefits of peaceful and mutually accepted relationships willingly entered into offer greater pay-offs in the long-run than permitting free rein to one's prejudices.

Furthermore, in a society of voluntary association, courtesy, respect, deference, and politeness become the social norms over time, and those who fail to act in such ways toward others (no matter how some of them might feel "inside") are faced with possible social ostracism or criticism for their "bad behavior." This reduces those individuals' chances for attaining their own goals and purposes for which they need the cooperation of their fellow human beings.

The Origin of Rightful Property and Its Justness

But a classical liberal philosophy of freedom and capitalism does not end with the self-ownership of each individual. It also argues for the right of individuals to establish a property right over "real property" in the form of resources, raw materials, land, produced means of production (machines, tools, equipment), and the finished goods manufactured from them.

It is based, primarily, on the idea of "first appropriation" or acquisition through voluntary exchange with others in society. "Natural rights" theory has long been controversial among political philosophers in general and even among classical liberal thinkers of various stripes. It remains, nonetheless, a core conception derived from John Locke that if a man settles down on land previously unoccupied or not owned by any others, that individual makes a legitimate claim to it as his rightful possession by in some way working and changing the land, such as clearing the field, planting the crop, tending it to maturity, and bringing in the harvest.

This idea follows from the intuitive sense that virtually all reasoning people share in common that there would be an inherent injustice or "wrong" if a band of thieves fell upon our land-settling and working farmer, and proceeded to plunder the efforts of his mental and physical labor. After all, our individual used his mind to conceive of transforming the undeveloped land into a farm. And he then set about producing the harvested crop through his own labor efforts.

If it is not his private property, then who can make a just claim to the fruits of his labor? The threatening band of thieves who now confront him? Some others over some neighboring hill who have done nothing to do the work to bring the crop into existence, but who say they "need" it for their own survival or pleasure?

If such a claim is made by either the thieves or by those others who just want his crop, what if he does not willingly part with this harvest? May they use force to seize it from him? May they threaten his life if he puts up resistance? May they kill him if he acts to retain possession of what his labor has produced? And if the latter, is taking his life if he defends his crop an unjustified killing?

If our unfortunate farmer does not resist the thieves because he fears more for his life if he attempts such resistance, imagine that he decides that this thievery is likely to happen again if he undertakes the planting and harvesting of a crop during the next season. He, therefore, decides not to do so, and simply tries to "live off the land" from what nature itself provides without any transformative labor effort on his part, so as to keep a low profile from the plundering eyes of these thieves.

If the band of thieves return and find nothing to plunder, may they physically take control of our luckless individual and, again under the threat of force, make him work the land to plant, grow, and harvest a crop for the thieves to claim as their own? If they do so, has not our individual been transformed into a slave, a person who does not own his mind and body but is forced to use them by the threatening command of others?

[…]

Income Inequality and Market Evaluation of Our Worth

But don't some in this capitalist system of division of labor and market exchange have more dollars to spend than I do? Can't they buy more and afford to pay higher prices than me and thus outbid me for some of the things I'd like to buy? Yes, this is true. But why do they have more dollars to spend in the marketplace than I have in my pocket? Because everyone else in society who has earned dollars to spend has spent more of them on the rich person's product or services than on mine. My fellow market participants have, in a sense, "voted" with their dollars and said they consider what that other fellow is offering to sell to be of greater importance and value to them than what I'm bringing to market.

All of our individual relative income and wealth positions in society represent what our fellow market participants think each of us is worth in satisfying their demands for things. Each of us helps in determining everyone else's relative income position when we spend portions of our own earned income on various goods we desire and for which we are willing to pay.

The capitalist system generates the institutional framework and incentive structure that leaves everyone free as an individual to live his own life, enjoy his personal liberty, and use his private property as his peacefully. But that very institutional framework and incentive structure of voluntary association and exchange in an emergent network of interdependent divisions of labor creates the setting in which it becomes in everyone's self-interest to primarily focus their knowledge, skills, and abilities in their production activities to satisfy the self-interested wants of others as the means to advance their own goals and purposes in society.

Where, then, is the "exploitation" of the workers or the consumers in such a "capitalist" society? Where are the incentives or capacities for "raping the environment" or hurtfully discriminating against people on the basis, say, of gender or race? What avenues are open and available for the less well-off due to birth or circumstances to better themselves and raise their relative income and social position in the community of humanity?

EVALUATING THE AUTHOR'S ARGUMENTS:

Viewpoint author Richard M. Ebeling bases his argument on the thesis that most people have the wrong understanding of capitalism. Does this viewpoint successfully address misconceptions, or is this tactic simply a way for the author to assert his own views of capitalism?

Capitalism Does Not Promote Morality

"These arrangements give capitalists the ability and incentive to behave in morally irresponsible ways."

Michael Schwalbe

In the following viewpoint, Michael Schwalbe argues that capitalism as an economic system promotes immorality. Schwalbe contends that people are not inherently evil but that capitalism naturally encourages less than noble behaviors. Moral hazard is endemic to capitalism, according to the author. Schwalbe also analyzes potential strategies to improve a flawed system. Schwalbe is a professor of sociology at North Carolina State University.

AS YOU READ, CONSIDER THE FOLLOWING QUESTIONS:

1. What is the concept of moral hazard as explained by Schwalbe?
2. How is an economy defined as capitalist according to the author?
3. Can regulation help the problems of capitalism as stated by the viewpoint?

"The Moral Hazards of Capitalism," by Michael Schwalbe, CounterPunch, September 1, 2015. Reprinted by permission.

In the worlds of insurance and finance, moral hazard is said to exist when one party to a contract or transaction feels free to take undue risks because another party will bear the costs if things go badly. The classic example is an insurance policy that protects against all loss or damage to property, and thus inclines the policy holder to treat the property carelessly, knowing that the insurer will pay in full for replacement or repair. Avoiding moral hazard is the alleged purpose of deductibles and co-pays. If insurees are on the hook for part of the costs of their risky behavior, the logic goes, they will take fewer risks and not exploit the insurer.

The idea of moral hazard gained public currency when critics of the banking industry used it to explain the financial meltdown of 2008. Deregulation, they said, created a condition of moral hazard that led to irresponsible behavior by all the powerful actors in the system.

Commercial banks had incentive to make risky mortgage loans because repeal of the Glass-Steagall Act allowed them to offload that risk by selling the loans to investment banks. The investment banks turned these loans into marketable securities and paid ratings agencies handsome fees to understate their riskiness, making it easier to sell them to credulous investors. More cunning investors, aware that many of these mortgage-back securities were junk, took out insurance policies that would pay off when massive defaults occurred. A history of federal government bailouts gave these banks and insurance companies further reason to believe that they would not suffer even if the whole scheme collapsed.

The situation was indeed rife with moral hazard. All the institutional players bet on an outcome in which the potential costs of their imprudent risks would come home to roost in other people's pockets. Which is pretty much what happened, homebuyers and taxpayers being left holding the bill. That deregulation helped this to occur is clear. In another way, however, the financial meltdown is not a special case. Moral hazard is endemic to capitalism; regulation just keeps it from crashing the system more often.

What the concept of moral hazard points to is how political, legal, and economic arrangements conduce to irresponsible behavior that causes, or poses a grave threat of causing, serious harm to others. Capitalism is precisely such a set of arrangements. It is not

As a result of the 2008 housing bubble and financial crisis, entire neighborhoods have been abandoned.

that some people behave badly because they're evil. It's that the normal workings of capitalism invite, encourage, allow, and often compel people—those who control the means of production and of finance—to behave in ways that cause great harm to others or put others at great risk of harm.

The political, legal, and economic arrangements that matter most—the arrangements that define an economy as capitalist—are private ownership and control of the major means of production; private control of investment; and the accumulation of wealth by extracting surplus value from other people's labor. These arrangements give capitalists the ability and incentive to behave in morally irresponsible ways. This is not a fanciful Marxist hypothesis. It's what we see happening every day.

We see it when capitalists cheat workers out of wages. We see it when capitalists hold down production costs by refusing to pay for health and safety equipment or pollution controls, thus risking the lives and health of shopfloor workers and of everyone living downwind or downstream. We see it when capitalists knowingly sell defective or dangerous products (cigarettes are the paradigm example).

We see it when capitalists extract fossil fuels in increasingly desperate ways that risk or create enormous environmental damage.

These are not deviant strategies in the capitalist scheme of things. The logic of capitalism requires, especially in competitive sectors of the economy, not only minimizing the costs of production but externalizing as many of those costs as possible and focusing on short-term returns. What this logic requires, in other words, is evasion of responsibility.

Capitalism's compulsions to immorality are also on display every time capitalists or their minions take the public stage and lie—about smoking causing cancer; about the health effects of pesticides, herbicides, and other industrial chemicals; about aerosols damaging the ozone layer; about climate change; and about their deep love for the earth. Acting in a morally responsible way requires seeking and accepting the truth about one's motives and the consequences of one's actions. But these are the truths that capitalists not only refuse to tell but vehemently reject whenever their profits and power are at stake.

Every form of exploitive economy, including capitalism, is built on a condition of moral hazard. This condition exists as soon as human beings are reduced to mere means to ends. People are "reduced" in this sense because what matters about them, in the eyes of their exploiters, is how much work they can do and how much of the value they create can be taken from them. What this condition invites is the treating of people as manipulable, disposable things, treatment that would readily be recognized as dehumanizing, were it not so normalized.

Feudal lords, plantation owners, and capitalists can, as individuals, be more or less cruel to the people whose labor they exploit. But personal demeanor does not change the character of an institution. If the profit on which one's survival as a capitalist depends comes from extracting surplus value from the labor of others, then one must constantly strive to reduce the cost of that labor. Most of what workers are made to suffer under capitalism—economic hardship, lack of autonomy and control, indignities on the job, speed up, deskilling, periodic or chronic unemployment—stems from this basic operating principle.

But it is not just "workers" in the narrow sense who suffer or are put at risk because of the moral hazards of capitalism. We are all endangered by cost-externalizing strategies that befoul the environment or warm the planet. We are all put at risk by unsafe and

defective products. We are all vulnerable to violent blowback from capitalist efforts to exploit natural resources, labor, and markets in other countries. We all risk being harmed when public infrastructure decays because government is starved by capitalists who, focusing myopically on their own enrichment, use their political power to cut or evade their taxes.

These vulnerabilities are of course not equally distributed; those at the bottom of the class ladder are at greater risk of harm. Awareness of this and a desire to avoid the worst that the system dishes out is what spurs competition to get ahead in capitalist society. This creates a secondary condition of moral hazard: incentive to treat fellow members of one's exploited class as competitors who must be defeated, or as resources to be used for one's advancement. For their part, capitalists have incentive to intensify this competition, if only by relentlessly touting the myth of upward mobility, because it divides and thereby weakens the working class. Here again capitalism reveals, in its bent for encouraging us to see others as means or obstacles to our own ends, its toxicity to morality.

An opposite view is often put forward based on the ideas of Adam Smith. In *The Wealth of Nations*, Smith argued that individuals working for their own gain are led by the invisible hand of the market to promote the social good. "It is not from the benevolence of the butcher, the brewer, or the baker," Smith wrote, "that we expect our dinner, but from their regard to their own interest." It matters not if these business folk intend only to get rich. The result, nonetheless, is a prosperous society in which people are bound together in harmony, as their desires for meat, beer, and bread are happily met.

Applied to transactions between small-scale artisan merchants and their customers, Smith's argument makes sense. But his philosophy is often mistaken to mean that pecuniary self-interest need not be restrained by other virtues. What Smith understood, as many of his modern acolytes do not, is that successful merchants must be able to see through the eyes of their customers and appreciate their desires not just for beef, beer, or bread, but for solidarity with respectful, trustworthy neighbors. It is this mutual sympathy, sustained by personal contact, that Smith argued acts as a check on immoral behavior more generally.

Proponents of the greed-is-good school of capitalist morality—most famously Milton Friedman—would have us believe that Smith's point about small-scale artisan merchants in 1776 suffices to legitimate the behavior of giant, impersonal corporations and investment banks in the 21st century. They would have us equate a baker's interest in making a living to a hedge fund manager's interest in making a killing. Of course the desire to do well economically can motivate constructive behavior. But under the conditions of moral hazard that obtain today, this desire, amplified by corporate power on a scale Smith never dreamed of, begets disaster.

Regulation is merely a palliative for the moral hazards of capitalism. Laws can forbid excessively risky behavior that jeopardizes other people's health and economic security. Laws can impose penalties for such behavior steep enough to make the risks not worth taking. But effective regulation depends on democracy; that is, it depends on the ability of ordinary citizens to use government to limit the potentially ruinous, selfish behavior of powerful economic actors. Which is why those same actors—today's corporate rich—oppose democracy in all but facade. Presuming that one sees democracy as a virtue, its inevitable decline as capital grows more concentrated and more powerful is another moral hazard of capitalism.

Taking a short view, there is no optimistic conclusion. A condition of moral hazard is part and parcel of capitalism, and so for now we are stuck with capitalism's inducements and compulsions to morally irresponsible behavior. What's more, trying to use regulation to solve the problem fates us to playing whack-a-mole, because capitalists, given the power that comes from ownership and control of society's major means of production, will always find ways to co-opt or evade whatever regulatory schemes and practices we might devise. On the other hand, struggling to limit the damage that otherwise unbridled capitalists can do is worth doing. Whacking moles can keep them from tearing things up as badly as they otherwise might.

Recognizing that degrees of moral hazard can be built into legal, political, and economic arrangements at least allows for optimism in the long run. The moral hazards built into capitalism can be built out of a non-exploitive, democratic economy. Such an economy would not require people to be socialist saints, always fully capable of the mutual sympathy that Adam Smith saw as essential to morality. It would require, more mundanely, laws, policies, and decision-making procedures that thwart the selfish, unlimited pursuit of wealth and power.

Even its defenders sometimes publicly admit that capitalism is a rigged game. The historical task, however, is not to try to unrig it, which can't be done. The task is to devise a more egalitarian game.

EVALUATING THE AUTHOR'S ARGUMENTS:

In this viewpoint Michael Schwalbe informs readers about the hazards of irresponsibility that occur under capitalism. Use examples and details from the viewpoint and your own knowledge surrounding the issues of either health or the environment and show how individuals might potentially suffer under capitalism.

Here's Why Capitalism Is Bad

"Capitalists make profits from global warming, from destroying our oceans, from pumping ever more chemicals into the atmosphere."

Gary Engler

In the following viewpoint, Gary Engler argues that capitalism is a terrible economic system. Engler backs up his assertion with ten specific shortcomings of capitalism and goes so far to suggest capitalism is a disease taking over the planet. He believes there is no hope for society unless we destroy capitalism. Engler is a Canadian novelist and journalist.

AS YOU READ, CONSIDER THE FOLLOWING QUESTIONS:

1. As stated in the viewpoint, how does capitalism negatively affect workers?
2. Following Engler's argument, is a capitalist society free?
3. According to Engler, how is capitalism destroying the planet?

"Top 10 Reasons to Hate Capitalism," by Gary Engler, CounterPunch, August 13, 2014. Reprinted by permission.

10.

Capitalist corporations suffer from a personality disorder characterized by enduring antisocial behavior, diminished empathy and remorse, and are rewarded by shareholders for acting that way. If corporations could be sent to a criminal psychologist's office they'd be diagnosed as psychopaths and locked away forever.

FAST FACT

A 2016 poll taken by Harvard University showed that 33% of millennials support socialism as opposed to capitalism.

9.

Capitalism encourages greed. But greed is only good for capitalists. For normal people it is anti-social and soul destroying, not to mention very bad for our communities, which rely on altruism, compassion and a generalized concern for others.

8.

Capitalism is a system of minority privilege and class rule based on the private ownership of means of livelihood. This gives a few rich people the power to buy and sell jobs, which means they can build or destroy entire communities that depend on those jobs.

7.

Capitalists praise freedom and individualism, but they destroy freedom and individualism for everyone but themselves. The vast majority of us who work for a living are daily asked to uncritically follow orders, to act as if we are machines, and limit our creativity to what profits our bosses.

6.

Capitalists denigrate cooperation and collectivism, but create mass production processes that rely on both from workers. Their system requires us to be cogs in a giant profit-making machine, but because they fear the power this gives us we are told working together for our own interests is illegitimate and bad. Thus capitalists undermine

Many argue that capitalism is to blame for the depletion of natural resources.

unions and other organizations that encourage workers to cooperate with each other and act collectively.

5.

Capitalism requires the largest propaganda system the world has ever known to convince us it is the only system possible. It turns people into consumers through advertising, marketing, entertainment and even so-called news. Millions around the world are employed to use their creativity to twist our feelings of love, desire, human solidarity and fairness into tools of manipulation, so that ever more profits can flow into the hands of a tiny minority.

4.

Capitalism is a system in which the principle of one dollar, one vote, dominates that of one person, one vote. Those who own the most shares (bought with their dollars) control giant corporations, many of which are more powerful than all but a few governments. Rich people also use their money to dominate the elections that are supposed to give us all one, equal vote. Under capitalism those with the most money are entitled to the most goods and services as well as the most say in directing our governments and our economy.

3.

Capitalism proclaims the virtue of naked self-interest, but self-interest without regard for morality, ecology or common sense leads to environmental degradation, destruction of indigenous communities, colonialism, war and other forms of mass destruction. Self-interest leads capitalists to seek profit absolutely everywhere, regardless of the damage done to other people and the health of the planet's ecosystem. Self-interest leads capitalists to destroy any rival economic system or way of thinking (such as indigenous communal land use and respect for nature) that can be a barrier to their endless quest for profit.

2.

Capitalism is not a friend to democracy but ultimately its enemy. When pushed, capitalists choose capitalism over democracy. If people use democracy to weaken the power of capitalists the rich and powerful turn to various forms of fascism in order to keep their privileges.

1.

Capitalism is a cancer taking over our planet. Capitalists make profits from global warming, from destroying our oceans, from pumping ever more chemicals into the atmosphere and from patenting everything they can, including life itself. Only by getting rid of capitalism can we rescue our environment.

EVALUATING THE AUTHOR'S ARGUMENTS:

In this viewpoint Gary Engler states ten reasons why capitalism is a bad economic system. Would previous viewpoint author Michael Schwalbe agree? Compare Engler's and Schwalbe's views on capitalism, greed, and the environment.

Capitalism, Communism, and Socialism— How Do They Compare?

"There is no purely capitalist or communist economy in the world today."

US History.org

In the following viewpoint, US History. org provides a brief description of the three economic systems of capitalism, communism, and socialism as part of their educational course on American history. This foundation will help you understand why the concept of moral responsibility would be applied to economic systems. The Independence Hall Association of Philadelphia owns the website ushistory. org and educates the public about Colonial and Revolutionary history.

AS YOU READ, CONSIDER THE FOLLOWING QUESTIONS:
1. As defined in the viewpoint, what is the means of production?
2. According to US History.org, who is the father of communism?
3. Following the viewpoint, how does socialism feel about wealth and income?

Karl Marx and Friedrich Engels turned the world upside down. Until the publication of their 1848 *Communist Manifesto*, much of the western world followed a course where individuals owned private property, business enterprises, and the profits that resulted from wise investments. Marx and Engels pointed out the uneven distribution of wealth in the capitalist world and predicted a worldwide popular uprising to distribute wealth evenly. Ever since, nations have wrestled with which direction to turn their economies.

Capitalism

- Capitalism is based on private ownership of the means of production and on individual economic freedom. Most of the means of production, such as factories and businesses, are owned by private individuals and not by the government. Private owners make decisions about what and when to produce and how much products should cost. Other characteristics of capitalism include the following:
- Free competition. The basic rule of capitalism is that people should compete freely without interference from government or any other outside force. Capitalism assumes that the most deserving person will usually win. In theory, prices will be kept as low as possible because consumers will seek the best product for the least amount of money. Does capitalism allow for government interference?
- Supply and demand. In a capitalist system prices are determined by how many products there are and how many people want them. When supplies increase, prices tend to drop. If prices drop, demand usually increases until supplies run out. Then prices will rise once more, but only as long as demand is high. These laws of supply and demand work in a cycle to control prices and keep them from getting too high or too low.

Communism

Karl Marx, the 19th century father of communism, was outraged by the growing gap between rich and poor. He saw capitalism as an outmoded economic system that exploited workers, which would

Karl Marx believed that capitalism was an inherently flawed system and hoped that communism would be an improvement.

eventually rise against the rich because the poor were so unfairly treated. Marx thought that the economic system of communism would replace capitalism. Communism is based on principles meant to correct the problems caused by capitalism.

The most important principle of communism is that no private ownership of property should be allowed. Marx believed that private ownership encouraged greed and motivated people to knock out the competition, no matter what the consequences. Property should be shared, and the people should ultimately control the economy. The government should exercise the control in the name of the people, at least in the transition between capitalism and communism. The goals are to eliminate the gap between the rich and poor and bring about economic equality.

Socialism

Socialism, like communism, calls for putting the major means of production in the hands of the people, either directly or through the government. Socialism also believes that wealth and income should be shared more equally among people.

Socialists differ from communists in that they do not believe that the workers will overthrow capitalists suddenly and violently. Nor do they believe that all private property should be eliminated. Their main goal is to narrow, not totally eliminate, the gap between the rich and the poor. The government, they say, has a responsibility to redistribute wealth to make society more fair and just.

There is no purely capitalist or communist economy in the world today. The capitalist United States has a Social Security system and a government-owned postal service. Communist China now allows its citizens to keep some of the profits they earn. These categories are models designed to shed greater light on differing economic systems.

EVALUATING THE AUTHOR'S ARGUMENTS:

In this viewpoint US History.org provides a brief discussion of the three types of economic systems: capitalism, communism, and socialism. Compare how the means of production are viewed in each of these systems.

Capitalism and the Free Market Are Great

Chris Berg

> *"The genius of capitalism is found in the tiny things — the things that nobody notices."*

In the following viewpoint Chris Berg contends that capitalism is more than the big flashy innovative companies and their products. Berg analyzes free market capitalism from the point of common everyday things and shows how companies are efficient and how they make things better and cheaper. Berg emphasizes that innovation and constantly improving already known products is what makes capitalism so special. Berg is a research fellow in Melbourne, Australia, working for the Institute of Public Affairs.

AS YOU READ, CONSIDER THE FOLLOWING QUESTIONS:

1. According to Berg, what two areas of business are most commonly associated with the success of capitalism?
2. What are two everyday items made better by free market capitalism as reported by Berg?
3. How is Ikea so successful according to the viewpoint?

Each year the glossy business magazine FastCompany releases a list of what it considers to be the "World's 50 Most Innovative Companies." This list is populated much as you would expect. In 2012 the leader was Apple, followed by Facebook, Google, and Amazon.com. Spot a theme? In the top 10, there are only two companies that are not primarily digital companies. One, Life Technologies, works in genetic engineering. (The other—try not to laugh—is the Occupy Movement. FastCompany describes them as "Transparent. Tech savvy. Design savvy. Local and global. Nimble.") Not only are most of them digital firms, but they're all flashy and unique, and they're almost all household names.

Everybody from *Forbes* to *BusinessWeek* hands out most innovative company awards. They're all pretty similar and predictable. But these lists have a perverse effect. They suggest that the great success of capitalism and the market economy is inventing cutting edge technology and that if we want to observe capitalist progress, we should be looking for sleek design and popular fashion. Innovation, the media tells us, is inventing cures for cancer, solar panels, and social networking.

But the true genius of the market economy isn't that it produces prominent, highly publicized goods to inspire retail queues, or the medical breakthroughs that make the nightly news. No, the genius of capitalism is found in the tiny things—the things that nobody notices.

A market economy is characterized by an infinite succession of imperceptible, iterative changes and adjustments. Free market economists have long talked about the unplanned and uncoordinated nature of capitalist innovation. They've neglected to emphasize just how invisible it is. One exception is the great Adam Smith.

In his *Wealth of Nations*, the example he used to illustrate the division of labor was a pin factory. He described carefully the complex process by which a pin is made. Producing the head of the pin "requires two to three distinct operations." To place the head on the wire is a "peculiar business." Then the pins have to be whitened. The production of a pin, Smith concluded, is an 18-step task.

Smith was making an argument about specialization, but just as important was his choice of example. It would be hard to think of something less impressive, less consequential than a pin. Smith wanted his contemporaries to think about the economy not by observing it from the lofty heights of the palace or the lecture hall, but by seeing it from the bottom up—to recognise how a market economy is the aggregate of millions of little tasks. It's a lesson many have not yet learned. We should try to recognise the subtleties of the apparently mundane.

Capitalism Means Efficiency

Ikea's Billy bookshelf is a common, almost disposable, piece of household furniture that has been produced continuously since 1979. It looks exactly the same as it did more than three decades ago. But it's much cheaper. The standard model—more than six feet tall—costs $59.99. And from an engineering perspective the Billy bookshelf is hugely different from its ancestors.

In those 30 years the Billy has changed minutely but importantly. The structure of the back wall has changed over and over, as the company has tried to reduce the weight of the back (weight costs money) but increase its strength. Even the studs that hold up the removable book shelves have undergone dramatic changes. The studs were until recently simple metal cylinders. Now they are sophisticated shapes, tapering into a cup at one end on which the shelf rests. The brackets that hold the frame together are also complex pieces of engineering.

Ikea is a massive company. Tiny changes—even to metal studs— are magnified when those products are produced in bulk. There is no doubt somebody, somewhere in the Ikea product design hierarchy whose singular focus has been reducing the weight and increasing the strength of those studs. They went to sleep thinking about studs and metals and the trade-offs between strength and weight. Their seemingly inconsequential work helps keep Ikea's prices down and its profits high. With each minute change to the shape of the Billy's metal studs they earn their salary many times over.

Being massive, however, Ikea has an advantage: it is able to hire specialists whose job is solely to obsess about simple things like studs. Ikea is well-known for its more prominent innovations—for instance, flat-packing, which can reduce to one-sixth the cost of shipping— and the extremely low staffing of its retail stores.

Franchises and frozen pizza brands have put a lot of time and money into developing ways to make their product taste as good as a pie that comes straight from a pizzeria's oven.

For big-box retailers, innovation is about efficiency, not invention. Extremely resilient supply chains may not win glossy innovation awards but they are the source of much of our modern prosperity. But Ikea is big and famous. So let me suggest another icon of capitalist innovation and dynamism: pizza.

Capitalism Tastes Better, Cheaper

Pizza is one of our most mundane and simple foods. It would be the last place most people would look for innovation and engineering. It is, at its most basic, a thin bread topped by tomatoes and cheese—a food of the poor of Naples exported, which is endlessly interpreted by the rest of the world.

Forty-one percent of Americans eat pizza at least once a week, whether purchased frozen and reheated in home ovens, delivered, taken away, or cooked from scratch at home. All of these choices are more complicated than they seem. Keeping a pizza crisp long out of the oven so that it can be delivered, or making sure it will crisp up in a variable home oven after having been frozen for weeks is anything but simple.

Moisture is the enemy. For frozen pizzas, this means that toppings have to be precooked precisely to avoid some ingredients being burned while others are still heating through. Frozen pizza takes a lot of abuse—it is partially thawed each time it is transferred from manufacturer to supermarket to home freezer. So the dough has to be precisely regulated to manage its water content.

Cheese freezes poorly, and consumers expect it to melt evenly across the base, so manufacturers obsess about cheese's pH range and its water and salt content. And of course all these decisions are made with an eye on the customer's budget and the manufacturer's profitability. The consumers of family sized frozen pizzas tend to be extremely price sensitive. The opportunities for innovation in processes, equipment, automation, and chemistry are virtually endless.

It gets even more complicated when we factor in changing consumer tastes. The modern pizza customer doesn't just want cheese, tomato, and pepperoni. As food tastes grow more sophisticated they look for more sophisticated flavors, even in frozen pizza. It's one thing to master how cheddar or mozzarella melts. Dealing with more flavorful brie or smoked Gouda is another thing entirely. Like Ikea's stud specialist, there are hundreds of people across the world obsessed with how frozen cheese melts in a home oven. These sorts of complications are replicated across every ingredient in this simple product. (How does one adapt an automated pepperoni dispenser to dispense feta instead?)

Customers demand aesthetic qualities too. Frozen products have to look authentic. Customers like their pizza crusts to have slight burn marks, even if home ovens won't naturally produce them. So manufacturers experiment with all sorts of heating techniques to replicate the visual result of a woodfired oven.

Takeout pizza seems easier but has almost as many complexities. Some large pizza chains are slowly integrating the sort of sauce and topping applicators used by frozen goods manufacturers. Cheese is costly and hard to spread evenly. The pizza chain Dominos uses a proprietary "auto-cheese," which takes standardized blocks of cheese and, with a push of a button, shreds them evenly across a base.

Moisture problems are even more endemic in takeout pizza. The cooked pizza has to survive, hot and crispy and undamaged, for some time before it is consumed. If the box is closed, the steam from the hot pizza seeps through the bread, making it soft and unappealing. But an open box will lose heat too quickly. Engineers have struck a balance. Vents in the box and plastic tripods in the centre of the pizza encourage airflow. Deliverers carry the pizzas in large insulated sleeves to keep the heat in but reduce risk of steam damage.

We could easily replicate this analysis for almost every processed or manufactured food in the typical supermarket. Then we could reflect on the complexity of serving food, not in a home kitchen, but on an airplane flying more than 600 miles per hour and 37,000 feet in the air, cooked in a tiny galley for hundreds of people at a time.

Some of the most extraordinary logistical accomplishments of the modern world are entirely unnoticed. Some—like airline food—we actively disparage, without recognizing the true effort behind them.

Capitalism Is About Innovation, As Well As Invention

One of the great essays in the free market tradition is Leonard Read's "I, Pencil." Read was the founder of the influential American think tank the Foundation for Economic Education. In his essay, he adopts the perspective of an ordinary wooden lead pencil and purports to write his genealogy. He began as a cedar tree from North California or Oregon, was chopped down and harvested and shipped on a train to a mill in San Leandro, California, and there cut down into "small, pencil-length slats less than one fourth of an inch in thickness."

Read's point: "Not a single person on the face of this earth" knows how to make a pencil on their own. The construction of a pencil is entirely dispersed among "millions of human beings," from the Italians who mine pumice for the eraser to the coffee manufacturers who supply their drinks to the cedar loggers in Oregon.

Read was vividly illustrating a famous point of Friedrich Hayek's— these separate people manage, through nothing but the price system, to make something extraordinarily complex. None of the pumice miners intend to make a pencil. They simply want to trade their labor for wages. Adam Smith's invisible hand does the rest. Read published his essay in 1958. The chemical formula for the eraser, known as the

"plug," has changed repeatedly over the half century since. The production is highly automated, and the supply lines are tighter.

Chemicals are added to keep the eraser from splitting. Synthetic rubber production in 2012 is much different than it was in 1958. These tiny plugs look pretty much the same but have evolved in a dozen different ways. "I, Pencil" magnificently captures the complexity of markets, but it doesn't quite capture their dynamism. The millions of people involved in pencil production aren't merely performing their market-allocated tasks but are trying to find new ways to make their tiny segment easier, cheaper, and more profitable. The pencil market—as far from a cutting-edge firm like Facebook as you could imagine—is still full of entrepreneurs trying to break apart established business models to shave costs and rationalize supply chains. In 1991 a gross of 144 simple, Chinese-made wood pencils sold on the wholesale market for $6.91. In 2004 that price had dropped to $4.48.

And this is before we consider the variety of pencils available to consumers — not just wooden ones of different shapes, sizes, colors, and densities, but mechanical pencils, jumbo sized children's pencils, rectangular carpenters' pencils (rectangular pencils can't roll away) and on, and on, and on. It is to capitalism's great disadvantage that there's nothing inherently exciting about pencils. Humans like novelty. We like invention. We like high-technology breakthroughs that will change the world.

I, Pork

The most insightful book about capitalism published in the last decade isn't a treatise on economics or philosophy but an art project. In *Pig 05049*, the Dutch artist Christien Meindertsma starkly shows photographs of the 185 separate products that are made from a single pig.

Every part of a slaughtered pig is sold and repurposed. Obviously, we're familiar with pork and ham but how many people realise that pig bones are converted into a glue that holds sandpaper together?

Or that pig fat is a constituent part of paint, helping its spread and giving it a glossy sheen? Pig parts are found in everything from yogurt to train brakes to photography paper to matches—even in bullets.

One response to Meindertsma's book is to see it as simply a modern-day reworking of Leonard Read's pencil. But it's more than that. *Pig 05049* reveals what a market economy tries to obscure: the deep complexities of individual products.

That single pig was stripped down and shipped to factories and markets across the world. It went into matches and copper and crayons and floor wax. These products are as mundane as can be imagined—what consumer spends more than a moment's thought on which crayon to purchase, let alone how those crayons are produced? But as Meindertsma points out, the distinctive smell of many crayons comes from fatty acids, which in turn come from pig bone fat, used as a hardening agent.

Pig 05049 was published in 2007. The oleochemical industry—that is, the industry that derives chemicals from natural oils and fats—is one of the most innovative in the world. Like any industry experiencing rapid technological and scientific change, it is restructuring as well, moving production from Western Europe and the United States to China, Malaysia, and Indonesia.

Six years is a long time in a competitive marketplace. As simple as they seem, those crayons are changing: costs of production have been shaved down, raw materials are being utilized more efficiently, and supply lines are being tightened. Amazon now lists 2,259 separate products in the children's drawing crayon category alone.

Government Doesn't Understand Innovation

If *FastCompany* has a warped view about the nature of innovation in a market economy, it is not alone. Governments do, too. The Australian federal government has its very own minister for innovation, and his Department of Industry, Innovation, Science, Research and Tertiary Education doles out grants for inventions and startups. Its Commercialisation Australia program sponsors inventors who "have transformed an innovative idea into reality."

Innovation Australia funds grant-seekers to turn their "ground-breaking ideas into commercial products." This is the invention fetish—the idea that technological progress occurs when dreamers have great ideas. All society needs to do is subsidize dreams into reality.

But ideas are the easy part. Getting things done is hard. Setting up a business, paring down costs, acquiring and retaining market share: those are the fields in a market economy where firms win or lose. The brilliance of the market economy is found in small innovations made to polish and enhance existing products and services. Invention is a wonderful thing. But we should not pretend that it is invention that has made us rich.

We have higher living standards than our ancestors because of the little things. We ought to be more aware of the continuous, slow, and imperceptible creative destruction of the market economy, the refiners who are always imperceptibly bettering our frozen pizzas, our bookshelves, our pencils, and our crayons.

EVALUATING THE AUTHOR'S ARGUMENTS:

In this viewpoint Chris Berg points out what he believes to be the good aspects of capitalism. Have you ever thought of everyday items like pizza or crayons to be so complicated in their manufacture? What other common items would you believe to be the same?

Chapter 2

Has Capitalism Become a System of Inequality?

Is capitalism to blame for the growing gap between wealthy businessmen and homeless beggars?

Viewpoint

1

Capitalism Is Far More Responsible Than Policy Decisions for Income Inequality

"In capitalist society it is much easier to make money if you already have money, and much more difficult if you are poor."

Ann Robertson and Bill Leumer

In the following viewpoint, Ann Robertson and Bill Leumer analyze the topic of income inequality in capitalist culture. The authors analyze the views of experts and report that inequalities in capitalism stem from the nature of its culture and the politics and policies contained in a capitalistic society. The authors expose specific examples commonly occurring in business and politics which back up their supposition that capitalism and politics cause inequality. Robertson lectures at San Francisco State University. Leumer belongs to the International Brotherhood of Teamsters.

AS YOU READ, CONSIDER THE FOLLOWING QUESTIONS:

1. Following the viewpoint's argument, what does an individual need to make money?
2. According to the authors what must business do to maximize profit?
3. As stated by the authors, how are politics and capitalism intertwined?

I n a recent New York Times op-ed article, Nobel Prize-winning economist Joseph Stiglitz theorized that capitalism does not inevitably produce inequalities in wealth. Instead, he argued, today's inequalities result from policy decisions made by politicians on all sorts of matters that affect people's income: the tax structure that favors the rich, the bailout of the banks during the Great Recession, subsidies for rich farmers, cutting of food stamps, etc. In fact, he concluded, today there are no "truly fundamental laws of capitalism." Thanks to democracy, people can steer the economy in a variety of directions and no single outcome is inevitable.

In their 2010 book, *Winner-Take-All Politics: How Washington Made the Rich Richer—and Turned Its Back on the Middle Class*, Yale Professor Jacob Hacker and U.C. Berkeley Professor Paul Pierson would seem to add additional support to Stiglitz's conclusion. As reported by Bob Herbert in The New York Times, they argued that "the economic struggles of the middle and working classes in the U.S. since the late-1970s were not primarily the result of globalization and technological changes but rather a long series of policy changes in government that overwhelmingly favored the rich."

Although there is certainly significant substance to Stiglitz's argument—policy decisions can have profound impacts on economic outcomes—nevertheless capitalism is far more responsible for economic inequality because of its inherent nature and its extended reach in the area of policy decisions than Stiglitz is willing to concede.

To begin with, in capitalist society it is much easier to make money if you already have money, and much more difficult if you are poor. So, for example, a rich person can buy up a number of foreclosed houses and rent them out to desperate tenants at ridiculously high rates. Then, each time rent is paid, the landlord becomes richer and the tenant becomes poorer, and inequalities in wealth grow.

More importantly, at the very heart of capitalism lies an incentive that leads to the increase of inequalities. Capitalism is based on the principle of competition, and businesses must compete with one another in order to survive. Each company, therefore, strives to maximize its profits in order to achieve a competitive advantage. For example, they can use extra profits to offset lowering the price of their product, undersell their opponents, and push them out of the market.

But in order to maximize profits, businesses must keep productive costs to a minimum. And a major portion of productive costs includes labor. Consequently, as a general rule, in order for a business to survive, it must push labor costs to a minimum. And that is why, of course, so many businesses migrate from the U.S. and relocate in countries like China, Viet Nam, Mexico, and Bangladesh where wages are a mere pittance.

This inherent tendency to maximize profits while minimizing the cost of labor directly results in growing inequalities. Stiglitz himself mentions that C.E.O's today "enjoy incomes that are on average 295 times that of the typical worker, a much higher ratio than in the past." In fact, in 1970, the ratio was roughly 40 times. C.E.O.s who succeed in suppressing wages are routinely rewarded for their efforts. Hence, not only is there an incentive to keep wages low for the survival of the business, there is a personal incentive in play as well.

While Stiglitz is correct in arguing that politicians can influence economic outcomes by policy decisions, what he fails to acknowledge is that these policy decisions themselves are heavily influenced by the economic relations established by capitalism. There is no firewall between the economy and politics. Those who have acquired money from the economic sector can then put this money to work in the political sector by lobbying and showering politicians with campaign contributions. Although politicians religiously deny that these contributions have any influence on their decisions, it is inconceivable that businesses—always obsessed with their "bottom line"—would continue these contributions without a "return on their investment."

Study after study has confirmed the influence of money on political decisions. The San Francisco Chronicle reported, for example: "In

US politics is heavily influenced by capitalism. Members of Congress depend on campaign contributions that may come with strings attached.

a state with nearly 38 million people, few have more influence than the top 100 donors to California campaigns—a powerful club that has contributed overwhelmingly to Democrats and spent $1.25 billion to influence voters over the past dozen years. These big spenders represent a tiny fraction of the hundreds of thousands of individuals and groups that donated to California campaigns from 2001 through 2011. But they supplied about one-third of the $3.67 billion given to state campaigns during that time, campaign records show. With a few exceptions, these campaign elites have gotten their money's worth, according to California Watch's analysis of campaign data from state finance records and the nonpartisan National Institute on Money in State Politics, which tracks the influence of campaign money on state elections."

Even beyond campaign contributions, political decisions are not crafted in a vacuum, remote from capitalism. Capitalism is a way of life, and for that reason it generates its own peculiar culture and world view that envelopes every other social sphere, a culture that includes competition, individualism, materialism in the form of consumerism, operating in one's self-interest without consideration for the needs of others, and so on. This culture infects everyone to one degree or another; it is like an ether that all those in its proximity inhale. It encourages people to evaluate one another according to their degree of wealth and power. It rewards those who doggedly pursue their narrow self-interests at the expense of others.

The culture of capitalism, because of its hyper individualism, also produces an extraordinarily narrow vision of the world. Viewing the world from an isolated standpoint, individuals tend to assume that they are self-made persons, not the products of their surrounding culture and social relations. So the rich assume that their wealth has been acquired through their personal talents alone, while they see those mired in poverty as lacking the ambition and willingness to work hard. People are unable to see the complexities underlying human behavior because of the atomization of social life. But the disciplines of psychology, sociology, and anthropology all concur that individuals are overwhelmingly a product of their social environment to their very core.

In 1947, for example, the American Anthropological Association argued in its Statement on Human Rights: "If we begin, as we must, with the individual, we find that from the moment of his birth not only his behavior, but his very thought, his hopes, aspirations, the moral values which direct his action and justify and give meaning to his life in his own eyes and those of his fellow, are shaped by the body of custom of the group of which he becomes a member."

It is in this more subtle way that capitalism induces growing income inequalities. Because of their intensely competitive environment, politicians are more vulnerable to this capitalist culture than most. Capitalist culture engenders a mindset among politicians that leads them to craft public policies in favor of the good people, the rich and powerful, and turn their backs on the poor or punish them with mass incarceration. They think it entirely natural to accept money from the wealthy in order to fund their re-election campaigns. And the more the inequalities in wealth grow, the more this mindset blinds politicians to the destructive implications of these "natural" decisions.

In 2011, Stiglitz wrote a compelling article, "Of the 1%, by the 1%, for the 1%," in which he argued forcefully that large inequalities in wealth are in no one's interest. But since then the politicians have continued to accept campaign contributions from the rich, socialize with them, and do their bidding. They ritually denounce the shamelessly low taxes on the 1%, but have done nothing to alter them. The culture of capitalism trumps logical arguments, and thus the inequalities in wealth continue to expand. Capitalism has an iron grip on the political process.

Stiglitz concluded his article with this prophetic statement: "The top 1 percent have the best houses, the best educations, the best doctors, and the best lifestyles, but there is one thing that money doesn't seem to have bought: an understanding that their fate is bound up with how the other 99 percent live. Throughout history, this is something that the top 1 percent eventually do learn. Too late."

While Stiglitz's arguments have had no impact on growing inequalities, thanks to the power of capitalism, nevertheless capitalism gets credit for producing the one force that can put a stop to these destructive trends: the working class. As Karl Marx argued, capitalism produces its own "gravediggers." In the 1930s workers massively organized unions and fought militant battles to defend their right to unionize and their right to fair compensation. These unions, which Stiglitz fails to mention, played a decisive role in reining in inequalities and unleashing a period in which the ranks of "the middle class" grew.

As Marx noted in his "Contribution to a Critique of Hegel's Philosophy of Right," "The weapon of criticism cannot, of course, replace criticism of the weapon, material force must be overthrown by material force; but theory also becomes a material force as soon as it has gripped the masses."

Stiglitz's criticisms of growing inequality will have little impact on policy decisions until they are embraced by the masses, the working class, those that capitalism cruelly exploits and who are so easily dismissed by politicians and academics. At that point the working class will finally stand up and collectively declare enough is enough.

EVALUATING THE AUTHORS' ARGUMENTS:

In this viewpoint Ann Robertson and Bill Leumer provide specific examples which seem to concur that both capitalistic culture and politics is the root cause of social inequalities. If you could change one of the practices spotlighted in the viewpoint which would it be, and why?

Capitalism Encourages Greater Wealth and Well-Being

Walter E. Williams

"Free market capitalism, wherein there is peaceful voluntary exchange, is morally superior to any other economic system."

In the following viewpoint, Walter E. Williams argues that capitalism is superior to socialism. Williams contends that young people think they prefer socialism because they are ignorant about the system. Williams claims that many Americans disparage capitalism because, ironically, it has been a hugely successful economic system compared to socialism. Yet many don't realize the brutality that occurs under socialism. Walter E. Williams is an economics professor at George Mason University and a columnist writing for the Daily Signal.

AS YOU READ, CONSIDER THE FOLLOWING QUESTIONS:

1. According to Williams how does ownership of one's self validate capitalism?
2. Why is free market capitalism disliked by many Americans as reported by Williams?
3. What is the brutality of socialism as stated in the viewpoint?

"Why Capitalism Is Morally Superior to Socialism," by Walter E. Williams, Daily Signal, May 30, 2018. Reprinted by permission.

S everal recent polls, plus the popularity of Sen. Bernie Sanders, I-Vt., demonstrate that young people prefer socialism to free market capitalism.

That, I believe, is a result of their ignorance and indoctrination during their school years, from kindergarten through college. For the most part, neither they nor many of their teachers and professors know what free market capitalism is.

Free market capitalism, wherein there is peaceful voluntary exchange, is morally superior to any other economic system. Why? Let's start with my initial premise.

All of us own ourselves. I am my private property, and you are yours. Murder, rape, theft, and the initiation of violence are immoral because they violate self-ownership. Similarly, the forcible use of one person to serve the purposes of another person, for any reason, is immoral because it violates self-ownership.

Tragically, two-thirds to three-quarters of the federal budget can be described as Congress taking the rightful earnings of one American to give to another American—using one American to serve another. Such acts include farm subsidies, business bailouts, Social Security, Medicare, Medicaid, food stamps, welfare, and many other programs.

Free market capitalism is disfavored by many Americans—and threatened—not because of its failure but, ironically, because of its success. Free market capitalism in America has been so successful in eliminating the traditional problems of mankind—such as disease, pestilence, hunger, and gross poverty—that all other human problems appear both unbearable and inexcusable.

The desire by many Americans to eliminate these so-called unbearable and inexcusable problems has led to the call for socialism. That call includes equality of income, sex, and race balance; affordable housing and medical care; orderly markets; and many other socialistic ideas.

Let's compare capitalism with socialism by answering the following questions: In which areas of our lives do we find the greatest satisfaction, and in which do we find the greatest dissatisfaction?

It turns out that we seldom find people upset with and in conflict with computer and clothing stores, supermarkets, and hardware stores. We do see people highly dissatisfied with and often in conflict

Free market capitalism is associated with glitz, glamour, and wealth, but it has other qualities that benefit us all.

with boards of education, motor vehicles departments, police, and city sanitation services.

What are the differences? For one, the motivation for the provision of services of computer and clothing stores, supermarkets, and hardware stores is profit. Also, if you're dissatisfied with their services, you can instantaneously fire them by taking your business elsewhere.

It's a different matter with public education, motor vehicles departments, police, and city sanitation services. They are not motivated by profit at all. Plus, if you're dissatisfied with their service, it is costly and in many cases, even impossible to fire them.

A much larger and totally ignored question has to do with the brutality of socialism. In the 20th century, the one-party socialist states of the Union of Soviet Socialist Republics, Germany under the National Socialist German Workers' Party, and the People's Republic of China were responsible for the murder of 118 million citizens, mostly their own.

The tallies were: USSR, 62 million; Nazi Germany, 21 million; and People's Republic of China, 35 million. No such record of brutality can be found in countries that tend toward free market capitalism.

Here's an experiment for you. List countries according to whether they are closer to the free market capitalist or to the socialist/communist end of the economic spectrum. Then rank the countries according to per capita gross domestic product. Finally, rank the countries according to Freedom House's "Freedom in the World" report.

You will find that people who live in countries closer to the free market capitalist end of the economic spectrum not only have far greater wealth than people who live in countries toward the socialistic/communist end but also enjoy far greater human rights protections.

As Thomas Sowell says, "Socialism sounds great. It has always sounded great. And it will probably always continue to sound great. It is only when you go beyond rhetoric, and start looking at hard facts, that socialism turns out to be a big disappointment, if not a disaster."

EVALUATING THE AUTHOR'S ARGUMENTS:

In this viewpoint Walter E. Williams argues that capitalism is morally superior to socialism. From your knowledge of history why was the National Socialist German Workers' Party immoral?

Fairness in Income Distribution Is Possible in the Free Market

"Fairness is a fundamental economic principle that lies at the very foundation of the free market system."

Columbia University School of Engineering and Applied Science

In the following viewpoint, the Columbia University School of Engineering and Applied Science describes research that attempts to use scientific principles and game theory to derive a way that will make possible a fair income distribution in countries. The author quotes the lead researcher who has analyzed European countries and found that some have already achieved a more equitable arrangement, especially compared to the United States. The Columbia University's School of Engineering and Applied Science is committed to bringing about innovative research that has a positive impact on humanity.

"What's Fair?: New Theory on Income Inequality," Phys.org, May 27, 2015. Reprinted by permission.

1. According to the 2015 World Economic Forum, what is the top challenging trend?
2. As reported in the viewpoint, which countries have a more equitable way of distributing income?
3. What unfair practices in the free market system are regulated by laws and watchdog agencies as specified in this viewpoint?

The increasing inequality in income and wealth in recent years, together with excessive pay packages of CEOs in the U.S. and abroad, is of growing concern, especially to policy makers. Income inequality was identified as the #1 Top 10 Challenging Trends at the 2015 World Economic Forum annual meeting in Davos last January. Columbia Engineering Professor Venkat Venkatasubramanian has led a study that examines income inequality through a new approach: he proposes that the fairest inequality of income is a lognormal distribution (a method of characterizing data patterns in probability and statistics) under ideal conditions, and that an ideal free market can "discover" this in practice.

Venkatasubramanian's analysis found that the Scandinavian countries and, to a lesser extent, Switzerland, Netherlands, and Australia have managed, in practice, to get close to the ideal distribution for the bottom 99% of the population, while the U.S. and U.K. remain less fair at the other extreme. Other European countries such as France and Germany, and Japan and Canada, are in the middle. The paper, "How much inequality in income is fair? A microeconomic game theoretic perspective," was coauthored by Jay Sethuraman, professor of industrial engineering and operations research at Columbia Engineering, and Yu Luo, a chemical engineering PhD student working with Venkatasubramanian, and published online in the April 28th issue of the journal Physica A.

Venkatasubramanian, who is the Samuel Ruben-Peter G. Viele Professor of Engineering, Department of Chemical Engineering, and co-director of the Center for the Management of Systemic Risk, has long been interested in fairness and inequality and points out that the

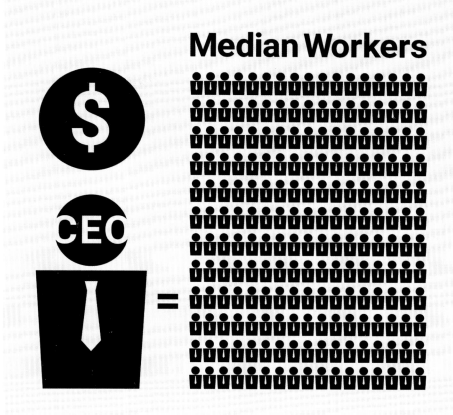

Median Workers

Thanks to bloated salaries and "golden parachute" deals, CEOs are paid far more than even the top earners in their organizations. Workers' wages have remained stagnant for decades.

same concepts and mathematics used to solve problems in statistical thermodynamics and information theory can also be applied to economic issues. A key element in his work has been taking the concept of entropy, usually interpreted as a measure of disorder in thermodynamics and uncertainty in information theory, and applying it as a measure of fairness to economics.

"Our new theory shows, for the first time, a deep and direct connection between game theory and statistical mechanics through entropy," says Venkatasubramanian. "This has led us to propose the fair market hypothesis, that the self-organizing dynamics of the ideal free market, i.e., Adam Smith's 'invisible hand,' not only promotes efficiency but also maximizes fairness under the given constraints. By defining and identifying the ideal outcome, our theory can provide an intellectual framework that could be used to design macroeconomic policies to correct for such inequities."

As an example of how his theory could be applied, Venkatasubramanian cites Switzerland, whose voters in November 2013 considered and rejected a referendum that would have capped the CEO pay ratio to 1:12. The number 12 was decided arbitrarily: Swiss activists felt that CEOs shouldn't make more in a month than what their lowest employees made in a year. Using this new framework, policy makers can now examine this topic in a more analytical manner and develop guidelines based on fundamental principles of economic fairness rather than arbitrary limits.

While economists have known that the Scandinavian countries have a more fair distribution of income, especially when compared with the U.S., they have not known how close to the ideal distribution these countries are, Sethuraman observes, until now: "It is interesting that the economies that are generally perceived to have a fairer distribution of income are also those that are closer to the benchmark income distribution we have found with our new approach," comments Sethuraman.

Venkatasubramanian has been pursuing a unified framework of game theory and statistical mechanics since he was a graduate student in 1983. This new work is the first to combine concepts from game theory, microeconomics, and statistical mechanics to address income inequality and the concept of fairness in an ideal free market environment. He uses entropy, which he says is a "wonderful concept that has been largely misunderstood and much maligned since its discovery 150 years ago," as a bridge that links statistical mechanics and game theory.

"This unified framework of game theory and statistical mechanics, which I call statistical teleodynamics, offers us new insights about both disciplines and answers some long-standing open questions in economics and game theory," he explains. "Economists have long wondered what it is that Adam Smith's `invisible hand' is supposed to be maximizing and what are the firms trying to jointly maximize in potential game theory. Our theory suggests that what the participants are jointly maximizing is fairness."

Venkatasubramanian and Sethuraman plan next to work with economists to conduct more comprehensive studies of pay distributions in various organizations, and income distributions in different countries, in order to understand in greater detail deviations from ideal conditions in the market place and improve their model.

"As we all know, fairness is a fundamental economic principle that lies at the very foundation of the free market system," Venkatasubramanian adds. "That's why we have regulations and watchdog agencies that punish unfair practices such as monopolies, collusion, and insider trading to ensure the proper functioning of free markets. So it is reassuring to find that maximizing fairness collectively is the condition for achieving economic equilibrium and stability. I'm excited to have a theory of fairness for a free market economy that is analytical and quantitative, and makes testable predictions that can be verified with real-world data on income inequality."

EVALUATING THE AUTHOR'S ARGUMENTS:

In this viewpoint the Columbia University School of Engineering and Applied Science profiles a researcher that believes in making income distribution in free market economies a fair proposition. From what you've read in the previous viewpoints do you think this is a good idea or even possible?

Viewpoint

4

"Companies should use their interactions with society to drive new business opportunities and create a source of significant untapped profits."

Companies Can Be Both Socially Responsible and Profitable

Floyd Whaley

In the following viewpoint, Floyd Whaley analyzes the topic of social responsibility in conjunction with business profits and sustainability. Whaley's analysis demonstrates two general ideas: some experts agree that social responsibility can enhance business, while others disagree saying that companies shouldn't be concerned about it, or that it might even damage business. The author argues that more research on the topic is needed. Whaley is a Manila-based correspondent and journalist for DEVEX, a media platform for the global development community.

AS YOU READ, CONSIDER THE FOLLOWING QUESTIONS:

1. According to the viewpoint what is the meaning of the phrase "shared value"?
2. How is the Taiwan-based Foxconn an example of a company in conflict?
3. What US business clearly links social responsibility to its profits according to the viewpoint?

"Is Corporate Social Responsibility Profitable for Companies?" by Floyd Whaley, Devex, February 20, 2013. Reprinted by permission.

In 2011, Harvard Business School Professor Michael Porter—the king of business gurus—put forward a radical proposition to global corporations.

"Businesses must reconnect company success with social progress," he wrote in the Harvard Business Review. "Shared value is not social responsibility, philanthropy, or even sustainability, but a new way to achieve economic success. It is not on the margin of what companies do but at the center."

"We believe that it can give rise to the next major transformation of business thinking," he boldly pronounced.

Though Porter's idea of "shared value" was warmly embraced by the heads of some of the world's largest corporations—all of which have active corporate social responsibility and sustainability programs—not everyone was convinced.

Larry Summers, the former U.S. treasury secretary, and a colleague of Porter's at Harvard, was overheard at the World Economic Forum meeting in Davos, not long after the announcement of the idea, asking incredulously: "Do you believe this [expletive]?"

Summer's offhand comment captured the core argument at the root of corporate global governance efforts. There is a wide chasm between those who believe that corporate social responsibility and sustainability are integral to company profits and growth, and those who believe such efforts are public relations at best and a distraction from core activities at worst.

"These conversations about corporate social responsibility and profits are held in silos," said Nigel Cameron, president of the Center for Policy on Emerging Technologies (C-PET), a Washington D.C.-based think tank that analyzes emerging trends in business and government. "The CSR people talk to the CSR people and the corporate people talk to corporate people."

"There isn't a connected discussion going on at a high level," he said.

The question of whether corporate social responsibility is profitable and adds value to a company is important to the development community because the private sector has far greater resources than government aid programs. If the game-changing resources of the world's largest corporations are put toward the tasks of poverty, climate change and other global challenges, the results could be dramatic.

Corporate social responsibility over the years has developed from a simple form of check-writing by companies to a complex set of principles that encompass nearly every interaction a company has with society.

"Corporate social responsibility encompasses not only what companies do with their profits, but also how they make them," according to a definition from the Corporate Social Responsibility Initiative at Harvard's Kennedy School of Government. "It goes beyond philanthropy and compliance and addresses how companies manage their economic, social, and environmental impacts, as well as their relationships in all key spheres of influence: the workplace, the marketplace, the supply chain, the community, and the public policy realm."

Porter's theory of "shared value" takes the concept of corporate social responsibility further. He argues that companies should use their interactions with society—and more importantly address society's problems—to drive new business opportunities and create a source of significant untapped profits.

"The ability to address societal issues is integral to profit maximization instead of treated as outside the profit model," Porter wrote in the Harvard Business Review article, which he co-authored with Mark Kramer, founder of the nonprofit consultancy FSG.

In the debate over the role that profits should play within the realm of corporate citizenship, the views on both sides of the issue can be stark.

Alice Korngold, a New York-based corporate social responsibility consultant to global corporations, echoes many of Porter's basic concepts.

"There is no question that companies that are the most effective in integrating sustainability in their values and strategy will be the most successful in increasing shareholder wealth," she said in an email interview. "Businesses that are the most innovative in finding solutions to global challenges—such as climate change and energy, economic development, education, healthcare, human rights, and protecting ecosystems—will be the most profitable."

The opposite case has been made by Aneel Karnani, a professor of strategy at the University of Michigan's Ross School of Business. He argues that by seeking profits and growth, companies generate employment and other benefits to society. They should focus on that task.

"The idea that companies can 'do well by doing good' has caught the attention of executives, business academics, and public officials," Karnani wrote in his 2010 study "Doing Well by Doing Good: The Grand Illusion." "This appealing proposition has convinced many people. It is also a fundamentally wrong proposition."

"If markets are working well, there is no need to appeal to companies to fulfill some vague social responsibility," he wrote.

As a practical matter, for those who make decisions associated with large scale investments in companies, the issue is more nuanced, according to Bharat Joshi, an investment manager at Aberdeen Asset Management in Malaysia who works with a team to oversee $1.7 billion in assets.

"If you ask us strictly as an investor, the key is that the company is being responsible on the social side but at the same time they have sustainable earnings, and it does not jeopardize the operations of the business," he said in a telephone interview.

"Companies should do CSR in a measured way, not funnel cash to a founder's social business or charity," he said. "It is okay to take from the bottom line if it is being done in a sustainable way. It's healthy and investors look at it quite highly."

Joshi noted that the relationship between profit and social responsibility is a more pressing issue in the United States, where companies place a premium on corporate social responsibility. Many large companies in other parts of the world, including Asia, need to focus on running their operations with more transparency before they try to improve the world around them.

"They must get corporate governance right, get their house in order first, before they address sustainability and social issues," he said.

Peter Gampel, the director of business valuation at the accounting firm Fiske & Company in Florida, in the United States, noted that a company's value is based on its tangible assets—such as it cash holdings, property and buildings—as well as its intangible assets.

Apple's products are produced at FoxConn, a factory known for its questionable working conditions that allow Apple to make incredible profits.

"If there is a merger, we are brought in to put a value on intangibles," he said. "There are dollar amounts for patents, licenses, customer relationships, trademarks, but we don't usually try to assess the value of a company's social responsibility. This is not quantifiable from a numbers point of view."

But, Gampel said, social responsibility does clearly have an impact on a company's value and profitability. Companies that are socially responsible make their brands more attractive to consumers and are more appealing to high quality potential employees. The impact on the profits of companies that behave poorly is less clear.

The situation of Foxconn, the Taiwan-based electronics manufacturer best known for making Apple products in China, is one of the clearest examples of the conflict between social responsibility and profit. Foxconn has been implicated in using underage workers and poor conditions at its factories have been linked to a series of employee suicides.

Despite the scandal, however, the sales of Iphone, Ipads and other Apple products produced in China have soared.

"If conditions were very dire and deplorable for the workers, consumers at some point would say maybe we shouldn't buy this product, but I think it will take a lot to get that point," said Gampel. "It will take a lot to get consumers to switch brand loyalty over social issues."

The situation is similar for investors, he said. They might be concerned about social issues, but it will not easily stop them from making a profitable investment.

"I don't think the social responsibility issues override the importance of profitability from the investors' perspective," he said.

The research on the relationship between profits and social responsibility is inconclusive. It indicates that large scale investors and the stock market do not clearly reward or punish a company based solely on its global corporate citizenship or sustainability efforts, though there are indicators of a slight profit benefit to doing social good.

The one thing that proponents and opponents of linking corporate social responsibility to profits agree upon is that more definitive data is needed. A key problem is how to gauge corporate global citizenship. Companies often have an inflated view of their efforts on the issue, and public relations is often inter-twined with social responsibility activities.

A 2009 working paper by the Bank of Finland looked at companies that were included or excluded in a key social responsibility ranking between 1990 and 2004, and the impact that it had on the value of their stock. The study found that stocks dropped an average 3 percent when a company was removed from a list of socially responsible companies. When a company was added to the list, its stock enjoyed a market value boost of about 2 percent.

In one of the most definitive studies on the topic, researchers from Harvard Business School, University of California and the University of Michigan reviewed 167 scholarly studies, according to a summary of their work in the report "Measuring the Value Of Corporate Philanthropy: Social Impact, Business Benefits, And Investor Returns," produced by the Committee Encouraging Corporate Philanthropy.

The study authors concluded that "after thirty-five years of research, the preponderance of scholarly evidence suggests a mildly positive relationship between corporate social performance and corporate financial performance and finds no indication that corporate social investments systematically decrease shareholder value."

The research indicates that the profit link to social responsibility could be vulnerable to other company activities. For example, global corporate citizenship might indeed be profitable but exploiting workers or destroying natural resources in developing countries might be more profitable.

The relationship between social responsibility and profits has not been demonstrated to the point that it is the primary driving factor in the way large scale, mainstream investments are undertaken. But there are notable efforts to go beyond socially responsible investing and bring in the hedge funds, institutional investors and other major players.

In 2006, then-United Nations Secretary General Kofi Annan launched the UN Principles for Responsible Investment, a set of values and guidelines for sustainable investing. To date, nearly 1,000 asset owners and investment managers—including many mainstream funds—are signatories to the program. Though the effort is worthy of praise, its critics note that the principles are voluntary. Asset managers can enjoy the prestige of becoming a signatory and ignore the principles if they choose.

Another more low-key but influential effort was established by the late actor Paul Newman in 1998. The Committee Encouraging Corporate Philanthropy was created to encourage companies to commit greater resources to philanthropy. Today, its members include the CEOs of some of the top global corporations, and it funds in-depth research into topics such as the links between profitability and corporate responsibility.

Though many are having the conversation about linking core company operations and profit to social responsibility, there clearly remains a large divide in the debate.

To illustrate this point, Cameron, the president of the Washington D.C. think tank Center for Policy on Emerging Technologies (C-PET), recalled a speaking engagement he had at the Planet Under Pressure conference in March 2012 in London in the run-up to the United Nations Conference on Sustainable Development (Rio+20).

He noted that the event was billed as a premiere gathering of those interested in issues associated with climate change, but there was almost no corporate presence at the meeting. The heads of the world's energy companies were also not in attendance.

"If the energy companies saw this discussion as part of their core mission, they would have been part of the process," he said. "It was mostly CSR people."

According to Cameron, the debate on whether social responsibility is profitable will not be answered by studies and research. It will be answered by the actions of the world's largest companies those who lead them.

"For most people at the top end of the investment community, the business community, the banks, the people who push the capital markets around, corporate social responsibility is a fringe issue," he said. "If the people at the top saw this as an issue of building long-term value, there would be a retooling of corporate resources and activities across the board. We aren't seeing that now."

Though the debate is far from settled over the profitability of corporate social responsibility, there is near complete agreement that corporate citizenship is no longer an option. It is now a requirement.

Corporate social responsibility is an intangible asset that in some cases is integrally linked to a company's profits—such as Starbuck's, which markets its coffee as beneficial to the growers who produce it. Its social responsibility in part justifies the fact that its prices are higher than a generic cup of coffee at the convenience store.

In other cases, social practices are more about risk mitigation. A chemical company might have little public profile or apparent need to address social issues, but if its waste fouls its surrounding community it will likely pay a price in litigation and government sanctions that affects its profits.

Companies around the world, and those who trade their shares and analyze their value, have recognized that corporate social responsibility has inherent value for a company. The exact dollar figure on that value may never be clearly quantified but the general trend toward greater corporate engagement in social issues is one that will have long-term impacts on the development community.

Viewpoint

5

"The fundamental problem of inequality is inequality between the capitalist ruling class and all other classes, but primarily the multinational working class."

There Can Be No Doubt, Capitalism Causes Inequality

Fred Goldstein

In the following viewpoint, Fred Goldstein contends that inequality is entwined with and is a natural outgrowth of capitalism. Goldstein's arguments are backed up by statistics showing the earnings of the top 1 percent of earners in the United States compared to the bottom 99% of earners. Goldstein contends that this economic inequality stems from the perennial struggles between capitalists or bosses and workers. Fred Goldstein writes on issues surrounding low wages and capitalism.

AS YOU READ, CONSIDER THE FOLLOWING QUESTIONS:
1. According to Goldstein, what is the slogan of Occupy Wall Street?
2. Following Goldstein's ideas, what is the scandal that has occurred?
3. How do the children of capitalists get wealthy as stated in the viewpoint?

"Capitalism and the Roots of Inequality," by Fred Goldstein, *Workers World*, February 29, 2012. Reprinted by permission.

The Occupy Wall Street movement has made the inequality in capitalist society an issue that has put the rich on the defensive, at least in public. The growth of inequality in the last 30 years, and especially in the last decade, has been talked about for years in many quarters by economic analysts and even some politicians. But before the Occupy Wall Street movement raised the slogan of the 1% versus the 99%, this condition went entirely unchallenged and was merely observed as an inevitable, undesirable (unless you were part of the 1%) fact of life.

The inequalities that gave the OWS its battle cry are truly obscene, reminiscent of the gap between monarchs of old and the peasant serfs. On the one hand, 50 million people live on food stamps, 47 million live in official poverty, half the population is classified as poor[1], 30 million are unemployed or underemployed, and tens of millions of workers live on low wages.

On the other hand, from 2001 to 2006 the top 1 percent got 53 cents out of every dollar of wealth created. From 1979 to 2005 the top one tenth of 1 percent (0.001 percent)—300,000 people—got more than 180 million people combined.[2] In 2009, while workers were still being laid off in huge numbers, executives at the top 38 largest companies "earned" a total of $140 billion.[3]

These numbers are just one reflection of the vast income inequality between the bankers, brokers, and corporate exploiters on the one hand and the mass of the people on the other. This has become a scandal, but no one made a move to do anything about it. So the Occupy Wall Street movement began its struggle in the name of the 99% versus the 1%. And it caught on like wildfire.

Since the fundamental moving force of the movement is the struggle against obscene income inequality, Marxists must give support to and participate fully in the struggle. But Marxism must also address this question and give it a class interpretation.

One can begin by asking the question: What does it mean to fight against obscene inequality of wealth?

It certainly means fighting to tax the rich and using the money to help the workers and the oppressed survive the economic hardships of capitalism. It means fighting for jobs. After all, being unemployed makes a worker about as unequal as you can get under capitalism.

The Occupy Wall Street movement saw protesters demostrating against the ills of capitalism.

Equality Within The Working Class
And Inequality Between Classes

Usually, when we think of fighting for economic equality, we think of the struggle for affirmative action in employment for Black, Latino/a, Asian and Native peoples. The fight for equality entails fighting for equal wages and working conditions with whites.

It also involves fighting for equal pay for equal work for women workers—i.e., for women to get the same pay as men for comparable work. And the fight for equality includes the struggle to ensure economic equality for lesbian, gay, bi, trans, and queer workers with straight workers.

Demanding equality for immigrant and undocumented workers with workers born in the U.S., especially with white workers, is an essential ingredient in building solidarity and advancing the class struggle of all workers.

Indeed, the struggle for economic equality within our class and between the oppressed and the oppressors is fundamental to building solidarity against the bosses. Inequality and division within the working class is both an economic problem and a dangerous political problem. It breaks solidarity and strengthens the bosses and their government.

But the problem of gross economic inequality in capitalist society is not fundamentally a problem of inequality within our class or between the middle class and the working class. The fundamental problem of massive inequality is inequality between the capitalist ruling class and all other classes, but primarily the multinational working class.

The inequality between the working class and the capitalist class is built into the system and is at the root of the question. So-called "excessive" inequality between the ruling class and the rest of society is constantly under attack, as it should be. But the general inequality between the ruling class and all other classes is taken for granted as a given and rarely questioned.

Inequality Built into Capitalism

That is because of the way income is distributed under the profit system. The income of the capitalist class comes from the unpaid labor of the workers in the form of profit, or surplus value. Everything created by the workers belongs to the bosses. And everything created by the workers contains unpaid labor time in it. The bosses sell goods and services and get the money for the unpaid labor time of the workers—that is, profit. They keep part of it for themselves and become rich. The other part they reinvest so that they can get richer in the next cycle of production and selling.

The income of the workers, on the other hand, comes from the sale of their labor power to a boss, an exploiter. The workers receive wages or salaries from the bosses. The amount is always kept somewhere within the range of what it takes to survive. Some workers are paid somewhat more than that and can have a degree of comfort. Many workers, more and more these days, get just about enough to live a life of austerity while others barely get enough to survive. Wages under capitalism are basically what it costs a worker to subsist and to keep the family going so that the bosses are assured of the next generation of workers to exploit.

Workers' wages always remain within a narrow range when contrasted with the income of the bosses. No workers can ever get wealthy on wages, no matter how high-paid they are. But the capitalist class as a whole automatically grows richer, even if individual capitalists go out of business or are swallowed up. The bosses continuously reinvest their capital and keep alive the ongoing process of the exploitation of more and more labor.

The bosses leave their personal wealth to their children as well as their capital. Their descendants, as a rule, get richer and richer from generation to generation, while the workers leave their children their meager possessions generation after generation. The workers have to struggle to preserve whatever they can through the ups and downs of capitalist crises and periodic unemployment.

How do you ever achieve social and economic equality under these circumstances?

In this context, for the OWS movement and all others who are for genuine equality, the question arises as to what exactly they are fighting for. If the ultimate goal is to reform the tax code, or to reduce corporate money in politics, or to regulate the predatory capitalist class and the greedy bankers—then the ultimate goal reduces itself down to a fight for a less obscene form of inequality.

That is certainly a progressive goal and should always be pursued as a means of giving relief to the workers and to the mass of the people in general. But no matter how you boil it down, if you limit the fight against inequality to keeping it within the framework of capitalism, then it means fighting to lessen inequality, but also to retain it and allow it. Extreme class inequality is built into the system of class exploitation.

Notes

[i] "Census data: Half of U.S. poor or low income," Associated Press, Dec. 15.

[ii] Jacob S. Hacker and Paul Pierson, "Winner-Take-All Politics" (New York: Simon & Schuster, Kindle Edition, 2010), p. 3.

[iii] Perry L. Weed, "Inequality, the Middle Class & the Fading American Dream," Economy in Crisis online, Feb. 12, 2011.]

EVALUATING THE AUTHOR'S ARGUMENTS:

In this viewpoint Fred Goldstein suggests that capitalism causes inequality as part of its system. If one reads between the lines it would seem that Goldstein would favor socialism. Would Walter E. Williams, a previous viewpoint author, agree?

Chapter 3

How Should a Capitalistic Society Change for the Better?

Can corporations do more to better society?

How Capitalism Could Be Good

"All of us— whether nonprofits, businesses, government, consumers, academics, and social enterprises— must contribute to fostering change."

Martin Whittaker

In the following viewpoint, in interview format, Martin Whittaker outlines important issues surrounding capitalism, how and why it must change, and inequality. The author believes the culture of capitalism does not encourage a focus on humanity or greater social good. Whittaker focuses on several key areas, pointing out ways that businesses could change—in privatization efforts, CEO's and shareholders, and technology. Whittaker is the CEO at JUST Capital.

AS YOU READ, CONSIDER THE FOLLOWING QUESTIONS:
1. What problems are caused by extreme inequality according to Whittaker?
2. How can CEO's change their way of thinking as outlined in the viewpoint?
3. Does technology cause inequality according to the author?

The World Economic Forum Annual Meeting kicks off today in Davos. Influential leaders in business, politics, civil society, and other sectors will come together to discuss some of the most pressing issues facing the world today—including climate change, technology, and inequality. To mark the first day of the meeting, JUST Capital CEO Martin Whitaker answered five questions about the agenda at Davos and the role of business in building a more fair and equitable world.

The high cost of entry to participating at the World Economic Forum means that vast majority of people attending are from the wealthiest one percent. Why should the one percent care about growing inequality in the world?

Quite simply, the one percent should care because morally, economically, politically and socially it is in their best interest to do so. Human progress and prosperity hinges on access to opportunity for all. Inequality that limits such access creates a vicious circle that fundamentally impedes our collective ability to build the kind of future we want and need.

Copious empirical evidence shows that extreme levels of inequality stifle economic growth (or worse, cause stagnation or recession), undermine productivity, and curtail progress. Over the past few decades, however, the conversation has become about more than money. Inequality is arguably a life-or-death issue. There is a clear and undeniable relationship between income inequality and social problems, including life expectancy, homicide rates, infant mortality, and much more. And according to a 2013 report published by the National Research Council and the Institute of Medicine, "On nearly all indicators of mortality, survival and life expectancy, the United States ranks at or near the bottom among high-income countries." Although the income gap is certainly not the only factor contributing to this worrying trend, we need to look hard at how it is affecting long-term health and well-being, and how we can use economic levers to help drive sustainable solutions.

At JUST Capital we stand for fairness, balance, and equality of opportunity; and for a market economy that allows all citizens to participate in ways that reflect their values.

The World Economic Forum, held in Davos, Switzerland, attracts such speakers as Canadian prime minister Justin Trudeau and Nobel laureate Malala Yousafzai.

One of the themes being considered at Davos this year is how new kinds of public-private partnerships might address issues related to the global commons. What is the biggest problem attached to the global commons right now, and how can we incentivize businesses and governments to work together to solve it?

The "tragedy of the commons" is undoubtedly a fundamental challenge of unchecked capitalism. But the forces that give rise to it are also deeply ingrained within the human psyche—and are an important element of free market enterprise. Areas with the greatest potential for public-private partnerships are those where the resources and attributes of each can combine to create a multiplier effect, whereby the outcomes are many times more effective than they would be absent such a collaboration. For example, the advancement of low carbon technologies is an area where the ability of the public sector to set carbon prices, apply early stage research and development capital, and accelerate distribution complements the ability of the private sector to bring innovation, capital at scale, business expertise, and efficiency to the table. Similar partnership benefits are clear in areas including Internet access, education, financial services, and food production.

All of that said, we believe that one of the greatest problems we face relating to the global commons is not any one issue but rather one of culture: In particular, a market culture that strips capitalism of any humanity and incentivizes and rewards short-term financial gain at the expense of the broader social good.

How do we break this chain? We believe at least part of the answer has to be getting more and better information into the hands of market participants, information that allows them to connect the dots about how acting with more enlightened self-interest can actually produce better long term consequences both individually and collectively.

In that vein, we believe that one way for the private sector to work with government is to help gather data, incentivize transparency, and require disclosure. The more the public knows about the issues that affect them and that they care about—from climate change and fair pay to human rights and taxes—the easier it will be for them to take actions that redirect resources to those providing solutions.

At Davos, Fortune 500 CEOs weigh issues that affect not only business, but society as whole. Outside of this gathering, though, most CEOs focus their time and attention on shareholder value. Day to day, how do we get CEOs to think beyond shareholder value and consider the broader societal impacts of doing business?

This is at the very heart of our mission. In our view, CEOs will only look beyond shareholder value if they are incentivized and rewarded for doing so. To do this, they need greater knowledge about what motivates their customers, their employees, their investors, and other stakeholders beyond just shareholders. In our conversations with executives, we see the pressure they face to maximize profits for their shareholders, often at the expense of other values. We don't believe that focusing exclusively on shareholders builds great businesses over time.

To bridge the divide, we are building a nonprofit market information platform centered on justness. It will use market forces to inspire and reward changes in how companies pursue a higher purpose.

At the heart of this platform is a new benchmark for business that measures and ranks companies based on how they perform on the issues the public cares most about. To understand what these issues are, we have implemented an exhaustive, multi-phase market research strategy—beginning with qualitative and moving into various phases of quantitative—that in 2015 reached over 43,000 individuals across the USA. Our research is a nationally representative sample that is mapped and weighted to the US census.

Each year we will publish the JUST Index, a list of the 100 most just companies in the country. We will also create actionable insights and tools that not only link justness to business performance, but also empower companies to improve their behavior.

Another major theme at Davos this year is technology, with particular attention to how it is reshaping all aspects of our lives and society. Is technology perpetuating inequality, or helping to narrow the gap?

The answer is both. Technology is just a tool: it can be used to produce and perpetuate any number of outcomes, both good and bad. And since the industrial revolution, we've seen how technological advancement fundamentally alters the relationships between labor and capital, between employees and owners. So this is not a new thing. To us, the real issue is ensuring fair and equitable access to technology and its benefits, and understanding the ways technology can be used to perpetuate or reduce inequality.

As such, there is a critical need for business and government programs that promote equal access to technology, that allow technology to be developed and deployed widely in support of human progress, and that stimulate innovation in the underlying forms and applications of technology. Knowledge is indeed power. And we are still in an era where access to information is transforming the way the entire world shares knowledge, whether in movement building, identifying and understanding problems, driving solutions, or simply helping to separate fact from myth.

If you were to take JUST Capital's mission and break it down to one core idea, it is that people—as consumers, business leaders, investors, concerned citizens, politicians, employees, or otherwise—will behave differently if they are given the right data to shape their decisions. And that could be incredibly transformative in reshaping our marketplace.

Is capitalism at odds with advancing social justice and tackling economic inequality?

In my #InequalityIs video, I talk about my time in Edinburgh, where Adam Smith, the father of capitalism, is buried. Adam Smith believed that humanity's pursuit of self-interest would naturally contribute to the social good. He believed that capitalism wasn't at odds with social justice at all. Today, I wonder what he would think. Would he change his views about the values of capitalism, or would he argue that something has prevented capitalism from taking its fullest form? I truly believe that capitalist ideals are not intrinsically at odds with social justice. At its best, capitalism creates opportunity for everyone, inspiring healthy competition and improving our society. JUST Capital is founded on the belief that the very laws of capitalism can be leveraged to help right the system. But if we are to solve the problems of injustice and inequality that have taken such deep root in our world today, we cannot afford to take a narrow or singular approach. All of us— whether nonprofits, businesses, government, consumers, academics, and social enterprises—must contribute to fostering change. And the more we work together, the more effective those contributions will be.

EVALUATING THE AUTHOR'S ARGUMENTS:

In this viewpoint Martin Whittaker outlines his ideas on how capitalism could and should change. Which do you think is the most important change and why?

Viewpoint

2

"The FTC supports free and open markets by protecting competition so that consumers reap the benefits of a vigorous marketplace."

To Protect Consumers, Promote Competition and Enforce Antitrust Laws

Abbott B. Lipsky

In the following viewpoint, Abbott B. Lipsky argues that consumers in America must be protected. Lipsky contends that by promoting competition among businesses and by enforcing antitrust laws consumers will reap tangible benefits. Lipsky outlines several tactics that the Federal Trade Commission uses to achieve these goals. Abbott B. Lipsky is a lawyer and former director of the FTC's Bureau of Competition.

AS YOU READ, CONSIDER THE FOLLOWING QUESTIONS:
1. How can businesses break antitrust laws as stated by Lipsky?
2. How did the FTC intervene in food service according to the author?
3. As reported by Lipsky, what impact does the FTC have on emerging product markets?

"Protecting Consumers by Promoting Competition," by Abbott B. Lipsky, Federal Trade Commission, March 6, 2017.

This is National Consumer Protection Week, a week set aside every year to help know their rights and make well-informed choices in the marketplace.

Here at the FTC, we're all about protecting consumers. One way we do this is by enforcing the antitrust laws. Competition is the fuel that drives America's free-market system. But competition can only thrive if firms respect the antitrust laws, which are the rules of the free market. When businesses break those rules—such as by agreeing to fix prices—they effectively steal from consumers and harm the economy.

The FTC supports free and open markets by protecting competition, so that consumers reap the benefits of a vigorous marketplace: lower prices, higher quality products and services, and greater innovation. Enforcing antitrust rules also allows businesses to compete on the merits, powers economic growth, and eliminates impediments to economic opportunity.

Here are a few examples of how the FTC protects consumers by enforcing the antitrust laws.

Prevent Mergers that Harm Consumers

The FTC reviews mergers to ensure that they will not lead to higher prices by eliminating an important competitor. For instance, the FTC stopped a merger between the country's two largest foodservice distributors that could have led to higher food costs at restaurants and cafeterias around the country.

Stop Business Practices that Keep Prices High

Any competition can produce winners. That is why a firm can lawfully become a monopolist by offering a superior product, better service, or more attractive prices than its rivals. But it is illegal for a monopolist to stop challengers from entering the market with lower-priced products. Last month, for example, the FTC required the monopolist of a critical drug used to treat sick babies to divest the rights to develop a competing drug. The FTC alleged that the company had acquired the rights just to keep any other company from

A HUGE FEEDER, BUT A POOR MILKER.

Uncle Sam (loq.). "If the beast cannot yield enough to fill that little pail, the sooner my stable is quit of her, the better."

This 1887 cartoon champions antitrust legislation by illustrating a monopoly dragon, "a huge feeder but a poor milker."

developing a lower-cost drug. The company also paid $100 million dollars in ill-gotten profits.

Promote Economic Opportunity

Looking for a new job can be stressful, but the last thing a job-seeker should have to worry about is a back-room deal among employers that would keep her from getting the job of her dreams or from being offered a competitive salary. As the FTC explained last year, the antitrust laws apply to job markets, and agreements among employers that would fix wages or other terms of employment for workers are illegal. Also, the FTC recently formed a task force on economic liberty to broadly examine the increase in occupational licensing regulations that may limit job opportunities, especially for low-income workers and military families who move frequently. Overly broad occupational licensing can limit employment opportunities for individuals moving to a different state, or prevent them from using vocational skills to open a new business.

Track Emerging Trends and Innovative Products

The FTC also holds workshops to bring together industry experts, consumer groups, and other stakeholders to share ideas and knowledge about new products or business models that could benefit consumers. Whether it's home-mounted solar panels or self-driving

cars, the FTC studies emerging trends to ensure that consumers are protected and competition flourishes in these new markets. In April, the FTC will host a workshop to examine how more competition and innovation might help consumers who need hearing aids, and the event will be webcast.

EVALUATING THE AUTHOR'S ARGUMENTS:

In this viewpoint Abbott B. Lipsky gives a brief overview of how the FTC works to protect consumers and writes that the agency is involved with new or emerging products. Explain how this might help consumers in the digital phone market.

Financialisation Is Wreaking Havoc on Economies

Rana Foroohar

"Even if we don't understand the particulars of Wall Street, we all know at gut level that the current system isn't working."

In the following viewpoint, Rana Foroohar analyzes a disturbing trend in economics. The author contends that financialisation has taken over and is causing a vast array of problems in business and economics, from giving too much power to shareholders and taking over corporate profits to creating too few jobs. Foroohar is a global economic analyst for CNN.

AS YOU READ, CONSIDER THE FOLLOWING QUESTIONS:
1. What is the name of the illness that plagues economics, according to Foroohar?
2. What are two ways that finance negatively affects people as reported by the viewpoint?
3. According to the author, what other country is adversely affected by finance?

"US Capitalism in Crisis While Most Americans Lose Out," by Rana Foroohar, *Guardian* News and Media Limited, May 22, 2016. Reprinted by permission.

Crisis always brings opportunity. And right now, we are having a crisis of capitalism unlike anything experienced during the last four decades, if not longer. The evidence is everywhere—in rising inequality, in the division of fortunes between companies and workers, and in lethargic economic growth despite unprecedented infusions of monetary stimulus by the world's governments (a huge $29tn in total since 2008). Eight years on from the financial crisis and great recession, the US, UK and many other countries are still experiencing the longest, slowest economic recoveries in memory.

This has, of course, diametrically shifted the political climate, creating a paradigm of insiders versus outsiders. In the US, Donald Trump and Bernie Sanders are different sides of the same coin; in Britain, Jeremy Corbyn is an equally dramatic response to establishment politics. The challenges to the political and economic status quo are not going away anytime soon. A recent Harvard study shows that only 19% of American millennials call themselves capitalist, and only 30% support the system as a whole. Perhaps more shocking, the numbers are not much better among the over-30 set. A mere half of Americans believe in the system of capitalism as practised today in the US, which is quite something for a nation that brought us the "greed is good" culture.

In some ways that is no surprise because, as I explore in my new book, *Makers and Takers: The Rise of Finance and the Fall of American Business*, the system of market capitalism as envisioned by Adam Smith is broken—the markets no longer support the economy, as a wealth of academic research shows. Market capitalism was set up to funnel worker savings into new businesses via the financial system. But only 15% of the capital in the financial institutions today goes towards that goal—the rest exists in a closed loop of trading and speculation.

The result is much slower than normal growth, which holds true not just in the US but in most advanced economies and many emerging ones. The politics of the day—populist, angry, divisive – reflect this, in the US, Europe and many parts of the developing world as well.

Shifts in the economy have wiped out America's Main Streets.

But the bifurcation of our economy and the resulting fractiousness in politics has become so extreme that we are now at a tipping point. And as a result, we have a rare, second chance to change the economic paradigm—to rewrite the rules of capitalism and create a more inclusive, sustainable economic growth.

Doing so will require a series of both technocratic and existential changes—everything from rethinking the nature of how companies are run (and for whom), crafting smarter national growth strategies and rewriting the narrative of trickle- down economics, which is now so clearly broken yet continues to guide the majority of economic policy decisions taken by our leaders.

But before we can do all these things, we need to understand where we are and how we got here. Our economic illness has a name: financialisation. It's a term for the trend by which Wall Street and its way of thinking have come to reign supreme in America, permeating not just Wall Street but all American business. It includes everything from the growth in size and scope of finance and financial activity in our economy to the rise of debt-fuelled speculation over productive lending, to the ascendancy of shareholder value as a model for corporate governance, to the proliferation of risky, selfish thinking in both our private and public sectors, to the increasing political power of financiers and the chief executives they enrich. All of which have led to a false sense of prosperity driven by market highs rather than real Main Street growth.

It's a shift that has even affected our language, our civic life, and our way of relating to one another. We speak about human or social "capital" and securitise everything from education to critical infrastructure to prison terms, a mark of our burgeoning "portfolio society".

Although the American financial sector dwarfs any other by sheer size, the UK is in some ways even more financialised than America, given the City of London's outsized role in the national economy. It's perhaps no surprise then that much of the most cutting-edge thinking on the topic is being done by Britons such as Sir Paul Tucker, the former deputy governor of the Bank of England, the current Bank of England chief economist Andy Haldane, and former FSA chair Lord (Adair) Turner. "The trend varies slightly country by country but the broad direction is clear: across all advanced economies, and the US and the UK in particular, the role of the capital markets and the banking sector in funding new investment is decreasing. Most of the money in the system is being used for lending against existing assets," says Turner, whose recent book, *Between Debt and the Devil*, explains the phenomenon in detail.

In simple terms, what this means is that rather than funding the new ideas and projects that create jobs and raise wages, finance has shifted its attention to securitising existing assets (such as homes, stocks, bonds and such), turning them into tradeable products that can be spliced and diced and sold as many times as possible—that is, until things blow up, as they did in 2008. In the US, finance has doubled in size since the 1970s, and now makes up 7% of the economy and takes a quarter of all corporate profits, more than double what it did back then. Yet it creates only 4% of all jobs. Similar numbers hold true in the UK.

How did this sector, which was once meant to merely facilitate business, manage to get such a stranglehold over it? Bankers themselves are often blamed but in truth the trend of financialisation was enabled by policymakers and the decisions they took from the

70s onwards, as postwar growth began to slow. In the US, interest rate deregulation under the Jimmy Carter administration, which was supported by a coalition of left and right political interests, led to the possibility of financial "innovations" such as the spliced and diced securities that blew up the world economy in 2008.

Reagan era shifts allowed banks and corporations alike to become larger and more financialised, and further Bill Clinton era deregulation threw kerosene on the fire. The legacy of her husband's laissez-faire economic policies is one reason Hillary Clinton isn't gaining more political traction. One of the most perverse effects of financialisation is that companies across all industries have come to emulate finance. It's no wonder—profit margins in finance tend to be much higher than in other industries, and the Copernican shift towards the markets has led us to revere the industry as the top of an economic hierarchy of services that we graduate to after passing through the lower phases of agrarian and manufacturing economies.

American corporations now get about five times as much of their revenue from financial activities such as offering credit to customers, tax "optimisation," and trading, as they did in the 80s. Big tech companies underwrite corporate bond offerings the way banks do. Traditional hedging by energy and transport firms has been overtaken by profit-boosting speculation in oil futures, a shift that actually undermines their core business by creating more price volatility. The amount of trading done by these organisations now far exceeds the value of their own real-world investments, a sure sign of financialisation)

British firms are very much a part of this trend. The recent history of BP (British Petroleum) is a perfect example not only of the rise of financial activities as a percentage of business but also of the perverse effect that financialisation can have on corporate culture: a focus on trading can lead to excessive risk-taking, and an overemphasis on short-term profit can undermine a company's financial future. BP was, from the 90s, an extremely balance-sheet focused company, becoming one of the most aggressive corporate costcutters of the era. This ultimately led whistleblowers to accuse the company of skimping on maintenance and using outdated equipment, even as it encouraged traders in its burgeoning US office to take bigger risks in search of trading-desk profits.

The strategy exploded in 2005 and 2006 when BP suffered a number of back-to-back disasters, including a refinery explosion in Texas City, Texas, an oil spill at Prudhoe Bay, Alaska, and accusations of manipulating energy markets via its US trading arm. In a move that echoed the manipulation of the California energy markets a few years earlier, Houston-based traders for BP US had used company resources to purchase a large quantity of propane gas, which they later sold to other market players for inflated prices, costing consumers $53m in overcharges. The company eventually had to pay back that amount, as well as a criminal penalty of $100m, and another $125m in civil charges to the CFTC (the Commodity Futures Trading Commission). The environmental disasters resulting from the explosion and Alaskan leaks cost tens of millions of dollars more in criminal and civil payments.

Since then, BP's Deepwater Horizon disaster in the Gulf of Mexico in 2010 became the largest marine oil spill in the history of the world, costing the company more than $50bn in legal fees, penalties and cleanup charges. You would think that all of this would have caused a serious crisis of conscience within the company. Yet far from pulling back and focusing on the core business, BP has charged full steam ahead into trading, becoming one of the largest non-financial players in the field. The firm now obtains at least 20% of its income from dealing in swaps, futures, and other financial instruments, up from 10% in 2005, the last time it disclosed profitability figures for its trading division. So where do we go from here? How do we curb the 40-year trend of financialisation and its perverse effects on business and society? Some people, such as the British economic journalist Paul Mason, are relatively optimistic. His new book, *Postcapitalism*, argues that we are at a tipping point in the process of financialisation, which has allowed capitalism to grow, like a virus, beyond its useful life span. He thinks that the technology-driven "sharing economy" in which information is freer and capital is less important will empower workers to fight financial capitalists in a new and more powerful way.

I'm less optimistic. In my own reporting experience, I've found Silicon Valley titans at the heart of the technology revolution to be just as rapacious and arguably even more tribal than many financiers. Uber looks to outsource, downsize and liquidate formal employees as much as possible. Apple, once one of the most admired companies on earth, is now one of the most financialised—over the last few years, Apple has issued billions of debt and made commitments to issue nearly as much as it has sitting in overseas bank accounts (some $200bn) to avoid paying more US taxes, and used the money to do buybacks that artificially jack up the price of its sagging stock. I think that changes in our current dysfunctional economic paradigm won't just happen but will require several shifts, both practical and existential. There is plenty of low hanging fruit to be plucked in the form of tax code changes that would incentivise savings and investment rather than debt—which is the lifeblood of finance.

We should reform business education to focus more on industry rather than finance (amazingly, given what we have been through in the last eight years, "efficient" markets theory is still the core of most MBA curriculums). We should rethink for whom companies should be run—workers, consumers and civic society as well as shareholders (many top performing firms already have that mandate). And we should certainly reform the financial system itself, reducing leverage, increasing capital holdings, and ending the culture of "experts" in finance.

Indeed, we should open the conversation about how and for whom the financial system should work to a much broader group of people—far beyond the small priesthood of financiers, politicians, and regulators who tend to share the same finance-centric view of the economy. "We need to stop treating banking as if it's a business unlike any other," says Stanford professor Anat Admati, whose book *The Bankers' New Clothes*, suggests a number of smart ways to reform and simplify the financial sector.

Finally, and perhaps most importantly, we need a new narrative about our financial system and its place in our economy and society. As the crisis of 2008 and its continuing aftermath have surely shown us, we are at the end of what financialisation can do for growth. We need a new model, one that will enrich the many rather than the few, in a more sustainable way. We need markets that are structured fairly, with the kind of equal access that Adam Smith described in *The Wealth of Nations*. We need a political economy that isn't captured by moneyed interests. And we need a financial sector that supports, rather than hinders, our economy.

Even if we don't understand the particulars of Wall Street, we all know at gut level that the current system isn't working. How could it be when 1% of the population takes most of the world's wealth, and a single industry that creates only 4% of jobs takes nearly 25% of US corporate profits? If we don't think hard about how to change things, the politics of the next four years may be far uglier than what we have seen so far.

EVALUATING THE AUTHOR'S ARGUMENTS:

In this viewpoint Rana Foroohar defines and analyzes the economic culprit financialisation. How does Foroohar think that Adam Smith, the founder of modern economic theory, would react to this crisis of capitalism?

Viewpoint

4

Let's Emulate These Socially Responsible Companies

Allison Gauss

"Companies are no longer content to do well. Today, many businesses also make it their mission to do good."

In the following viewpoint, Allison Gauss contends that businesses can be successful and profitable and have a mission to do good at the same time. The author profiles six companies that are leaders in the area of corporate social responsibility and emphasizes the importance of supporting such companies. Allison Gauss is a freelance writer.

AS YOU READ, CONSIDER THE FOLLOWING QUESTIONS:

1. As defined in the viewpoint, what is corporate social responsibility?
2. According to Gauss, which global company supports the World Wildlife Fund?
3. Which company is concerned about water supplies as reported in the viewpoint?

"6 Socially Responsible Companies to Applaud," by Allison Gauss, Classy, Inc, May 11, 2018. Reprinted by permission.

Companies are no longer content to do well. Today, many businesses also make it their mission to do good. Corporate social responsibility (CSR) refers to this growing practice of for-profit organizations aligning with relevant causes and social good programs.

Social responsibility, beyond making the world a better place, also benefits companies in their recruiting and consumer marketing efforts. The Nielsen Global Survey of Corporate Social Responsibility found that more than half of people surveyed "are willing to pay more for products and services provided by companies that are committed to positive social and environmental impact" and two-thirds would rather work for such a company.

It's important to recognize and celebrate socially responsible companies, both to encourage their work and to show other organizations how they can successfully incorporate social good into their mission. These are some of the most progressive and impactful for-profits contributing to positive social change. If you're unable to give a solid answer or examples when someone asks, "What is corporate social responsibility?," then check out the following programs. Use this inspiration to work across sectors and partner with companies who care.

1. Google

Besides being the world's most popular search engine, Google also achieved its 100 percent renewable energy target in 2017, and is now the largest corporate renewable energy purchaser on the planet.

As if that wasn't enough to earn a spot at the top of the corporate social responsibility totem pole, the company also provides grants to several dedicated social impact initiatives, including the Equal Justice Initiative, Goodwill Industries International, and Pratham Books: StoryWeaver platform.

From facilitating green commuting, to employee gift matching, to paid time off to volunteer, Google inspects nearly every part of their business with a social impact lens.

Takeaway: You can have a positive social impact in all kinds of ways. Looking to go green? Evaluate how your organization uses

Ben & Jerry's doesn't only make delicious ice cream. They are a socially conscious certified B company with a mission to balance profit and purpose.

energy and other resources and introduce simple changes to make your business more environmentally friendly.

2. Ben & Jerry's

Ice cream tastes just a little sweeter when you know the makers work to promote safe, socially responsible ingredients and business practices. Since the 1980s, Ben & Jerry's has supported a number of important causes, many of which are directly tied to the business of making ice cream.

In 1989, they first opposed recombinant bovine growth hormone use in cows, in part due to "its adverse economic impact on family farming." They have also used their packaging to support the family farm organization, Farm Aid. The company even created the

Ben & Jerry's Foundation, which encourages their employees to give back to their communities and offers grants for social justice programs.

Takeaway: Every industry faces decisions about whether to prioritize values over profit. Ben & Jerry's makes socially responsible decisions regarding the farming and dairy industries. Ask what choices your business faces and remember to bring your values and ideals into difficult conversations.

3. LEGO

The LEGO Group is one of the most notable examples of how social responsibility can be an incredible asset to a well-known brand. Their dedication to social impact is somewhat recent (a 2014 Greenpeace video put pressure on the toymaker to end their 50-year partnership with Shell Global due to their plans to drill in the Arctic), but the extent of their commitment has made the Danish company a shining example of the far-reaching impact of CSR.

The company was recently slated as one of the top examples of social responsibility by Reputation Institute and ranked second for Reputation Institute's RepTrak 100—which lists the most highly-regarded companies in the world.

In addition to partnerships with organizations like the World Wildlife Fund, LEGO has also made a commitment to reduce their carbon footprint and is working towards 100 percent renewable energy capacity by 2030. The behemoth business has baked environmentally friendly processes into their manufacturing with the creation of LEGO's Sustainable Materials Center, which works to find sustainable alternatives to their current materials and packaging.

LEGO has also made a public commitment to ethical business practices and high standards for human rights for their employees.

Takeaway: It's never too late to make a difference. Even the slightest effort towards social change can have a positive impact on the world and encourage other businesses to do the same.

4. Levi Strauss

Are your jeans contributing to water scarcity? Most of us probably don't think about this when shopping, but it's an important question for Levi Strauss. In recent years, the company has committed to reducing the amount of water used in production of their jeans, a product they have been making since 1873.

According to Levi Strauss's website, their way of designing and manufacturing has saved more than 1 billion liters of water since its inception in 2011. The company has also worked to fight stigma and support people living with HIV/AIDS, facilitate clothing recycling with Goodwill, and decrease their contribution to climate change.

Takeaway: Even the oldest companies and industries can adapt and innovate for social good. Manufacturing is an important part of operations where companies should look for opportunities to improve. Producing goods in a socially responsible way is a vital element of CSR.

5. Warby Parker

For people in the developed world, the need for a new pair of glasses is a chance to accessorize, but it can also be a chore to find the right ones. Warby Parker helps simplify the task by sending customers five different frames of their choice to try on before making a decision. But knowing that for many people a functional pair of glasses can be life-changing, the B-Corp also works to provide glasses for those in need.

Through their Buy-A-Pair, Give-A-Pair program, Warby Parker makes a monthly donation to their nonprofit partners, such as VisionSpring, to bring prescription eyewear to people in developing countries. The company has distributed more than four million pairs of glasses since its start in 2010.

Takeaway: Giving back doesn't have to be just an ancillary benefit. The advent of B-Corps and the popularity of CSR means that for-profit businesses have more opportunity than ever to exact social change. Now is the perfect time to reevaluate your company's mission and build social good into the foundation of your business.

6. Microsoft

Microsoft changed the way the world works, studies, and plays with their computers and software. But their ambitions go far beyond the screen. The company, founded by Bill Gates who now devotes his time to philanthropy, began its giving program in 1983 when the fledgling company raised $17,000 for charity. As their philanthropy webpage explains, Microsoft's giving program has not only given time (employees have spent five million hours volunteering in the last 13 years) but also cash. The program reached a total of $1.6 billion given in 2017 and is on track to reach $2 billion by 2020.

The software giant also created Microsoft Philanthropies, a social good initiative that works with nonprofits, governments, and businesses to create "a future where every person has the skills, knowledge, and opportunity to achieve more." Initiatives cover everything from providing computer education, offering grants to nonprofits, and forming partnerships with organizations around the world.

Takeaway: CSR can grow with your business. While your organization's contribution to a cause may start small, it plants the seed of philanthropy in your culture. Even small or brand new businesses can find a way to give back. In time, their commitment to social responsibility can have big impact.

More and more companies are not only adopting causes and social good initiatives but also building them into the framework of their businesses. These organizations show how far-reaching and varied corporate social responsibility programs can be.

Whether it's donating your product to those in need, fundraising for a worthy cause, or starting your own foundation, any business can prioritize social impact. Along with the good it does for your community, it also benefits your brand and attracts customers and talented employees.

Perhaps the simplest way to take a philanthropic step is to sponsor a local nonprofit organization. Corporate sponsorships between nonprofits and for-profit businesses can take many forms, so download The Nonprofit's Guide to Pitching to Corporate Sponsors to learn where to get started.

EVALUATING THE AUTHOR'S ARGUMENTS:

In this viewpoint Allison Gauss profiles six companies that are given good marks on the corporate social responsibility report card. Would this knowledge affect your buying choices? Give details from the viewpoint to back up your response.

Viewpoint
5

Supporting Humanitarian Aid Makes Good Business Sense

"Forward-thinking companies now look to bring their core capabilities to a humanitarian crisis."

Megan Schumann, Alex Haseley, and Frank Clary

In the following viewpoint, Megan Schumann, Alex Haseley, and Frank Clary analyze how businesses are partnering with humanitarian agencies to provide relief to crises around the globe. The authors detail specific companies and their partnerships and argue why businesses should help out and how private businesses can get started in this area. Schumann is a senior consultant for social impact consulting at Deloitte. Haseley is a senior manager for strategic risk at Deloitte. Clary is a director for corporate social responsibility at Agility.

AS YOU READ, CONSIDER THE FOLLOWING QUESTIONS:

1. As defined by this viewpoint, what are "complex crises?"
2. How does Coca-Cola support humanitarian efforts according to the authors?
3. Why should private business become involved in humanitarian efforts according to the author?

"Why Supporting Humanitarian Aid Makes Business Sense," by Megan Schumann, Alex Haseley and Frank Clary, World Economic Forum, May 20, 2016. Reprinted by permission.

L ast year, a photo of toddler Alan Kurdi's body on a Turkish beach evoked a global reaction to the plight of Syrian refugees. The business community was quick to respond, donating an unprecedented $17 million to refugee aid in one week. Perhaps more striking than the scale and speed of corporate contributions is that they increasingly go beyond cash. Forward-thinking companies now look to bring their core capabilities to a humanitarian crisis, and are laying the groundwork to do so by establishing partnerships before crises hit.

Many of today's crises combine economic, social, political, and environmental conflict, warranting the label "complex crises." These interconnected issues may exceed what traditional humanitarian organizations can address. Complex crises also carry significant implications for businesses and economies, often motivating private sector involvement.

While committing to support a crisis is a big decision for a company, determining how to contribute beyond financial donations is even more daunting. This article looks at how companies are teaming up with humanitarian organizations to address complex crises. It draws on 30+ interviews with companies, humanitarian organizations, and academics, and is part of ongoing research by the World Economic Forum and Deloitte to improve the assistance provided to those impacted by crises.

Partnerships for Tackling Crises

The humanitarian organizations interviewed made it clear that when companies choose not to collaborate, it may actually be counterproductive to crisis response efforts. For instance, the donation of unnecessary and unrequested supplies, known as Unsolicited Bilateral Donations, can lead to supplies going unused and clogging up main transportation channels.

As a result, many companies are seeking out partners that are familiar with the nuances of the humanitarian system. Corporate-humanitarian partnerships fell into three distinct types, with some companies engaging in multiple types of partnership.

Interview participants often find projects to be an ideal way of experimenting with new partners, with 75% of businesses interviewed

Many corporations are partnering with humanitarian organizations to address global crises.

engaging in them. Companies cite flexibility as a major advantage of this form of partnership. A project can be tailored to the conditions of a specific crisis, and concluded once the desired outcome is achieved. When these collaborations are successful, they can be adapted to fit the needs of a new crisis.

For example, Coca-Cola recognized an opportunity to leverage its local relationships during the 2014 Ebola outbreak and embarked on a crisis-specific project. The company partnered with communications coalition Africa United on a public education campaign to halt the spread of Ebola. Africa United designed a messaging campaign across various mediums, including notebooks, posters and trading cards with celebrity soccer stars and public health messaging. The local Coca-Cola bottling partner supported printing and distribution of the materials to NGO partners for use in broader education efforts.

The growing trust between humanitarian organizations and companies has increased the popularity of sustained partnerships. More time working together helps identify and make the most of each partner's unique capabilities. "Companies use the mentality of 'practice makes perfect' since most businesses are successful by doing what they excel at over and over again," reflects Paul Musser of MasterCard. "Bringing that level of reliability to our work with humanitarian organizations is what builds trust. It enables us to work together through different crises."

As partnerships with humanitarian organizations blossom, the desire to widen the circle of collaborators and learn from others' efforts leads to knowledge networks. Global logistics companies Maersk, UPS and Agility coordinate their crisis response efforts through the Logistics Emergency Team (LET), which supports the Logistics Cluster led by the United Nations World Food Programme. Each company has its own set of partnerships beyond the LET that can be activated to respond to a need. For instance, UPS has a partnership with Gavi, the vaccine alliance, and robotics company Zipline enabling it to deliver vaccines and blood via drone. When companies pool their expertise it can be a relatively light lift for each company that results in an outsized impact in the crisis.

However, these networks are still in short supply, as only 20% of companies interviewed are currently active in one. Those that exist have struggled to scale beyond a few active members. More are needed, including ones that engage companies beyond the telecom, logistics, and health sectors currently served by existing networks.

Why Businesses Should Help

"We can't be a global, multicultural company without contributing to global issues," said Charles Mouzannar of Amec Foster Wheeler, an international construction company. Many global companies recognize that supporting complex crises is essential to their values and reputation. They also understand how it can mitigate business risks and support economic growth where they operate. As part of its MasterCard Aid Network, MasterCard partnered with Save the Children to provide chip-enabled cash vouchers to people affected by civil unrest in Yemen. This initiative reflects a long term commitment to financial inclusion that positions MasterCard to be a part of Yemen's economic recovery.

Contributing towards local employment and strengthening local communities have become priorities for companies like Amec Foster Wheeler that plan to work in fragile regions for many years to come, and want to draw from a strong local talent pool.

A company's ongoing role in a fragile region can also help stabilize the economic activity in the area, supporting the region's resilience and recovery. During the Ebola crisis, Maersk worked closely with affected countries' authorities to help make sure that Maersk-operated ports remained open, and that Maersk vessels continued to call on ports in Guinea, Liberia and Sierra Leone. These actions helped maintain the flow of essential supplies, and kept the costs of in-demand products lower than they might be otherwise.

What Can You Do?

With more than 100 million people in the world affected by humanitarian crises, there is no better time for the private sector to strengthen its engagement. The private sector has proven itself to be a reliable and valuable partner, but the full scale of its potential is yet to be realized. Achieving meaningful, long-term impact starts with teaming with humanitarian partners on the ground long before a crisis arises.

Recent crises have underscored this fact. As Allison Neale of Henry Schein, a global provider of healthcare products and services, reflects, "the Ebola crisis highlighted that we must improve how we collectively respond to crises. We'll be faster and more effective if we have partnerships between the public and private sectors established well in advance of crises."

Consider how your company could be involved. Will you start with a project, engage in a sustained partnership, or join a knowledge sharing network? Companies of all types are rallying to address complex crises. Every company is invited to contribute and activate its business network to address these pressing challenges.

EVALUATING THE AUTHORS' ARGUMENTS:

In this viewpoint the authors detail how companies are partnering with humanitarian agencies to bring relief to crises around the world. Construct an argument to convince someone who might not agree with the idea of businesses engaging in social responsibility.

Facts About Capitalism and Moral Responsibility

Editor's note: These facts can be used in reports to add credibility when making important points or claims.

Important Definitions

Capitalism: An economic system in which most property is privately owned (by individuals or businesses) and the production (as in factories and offices) of goods and services, as well as the distribution of income and wealth, are largely determined by the operation of free markets.

Socialism: A political and economic system in which most forms of valuable property and resources are owned or controlled by the public or the state. In a strictly socialist economy, public agencies influence and may decide what kinds of goods and services are produced, how much they cost, the wages or salaries paid to people in different professions, and how much wealth a single individual may accumulate. Most socialist systems also provide citizens with significant social benefits (such as health care, child care, and education).

Communism: A political and economic system in which the major resources of production (such as farms and factories) are owned by the public or the state, and wealth is divided among citizens equally or according to individual need. It is one form of socialism.

Morality or Ethics: Most societies, from ancient to modern, share certain codes of behavior. These include customs or laws forbidding murder, bodily injury, or attacks on personal honor and reputation. Property rights are also found almost everywhere. In societies where Judaism, Christianity, Islam, and Buddhism are common religions people usually feel a duty to help the needy, tell the truth and keep promises

Universal moral values for corporate entities: Six universal moral values for corporate codes of ethics have been proposed and include: trustworthiness, respect, responsibility, fairness, caring, and citizenship.

Important People
Adam Smith: Considered to be the father of modern economics. His 1776 book, *The Wealth of Nations,* lays the foundation for modern economic thought.

Karl Marx: Considered to be the father of communism. With Friedrich Engels he wrote and published the *Communist Manifesto* in 1848.

Popular Protest Movements
Occupy Wall Street—Began in September 2011, to protest what was seen as the negatives of capitalism including the excessive power of banks, multinational corporations, and Wall Street.

"Fight for $15"—Began in 2012 to protest low minimum wages for workers in fast food, home health care, retail, and others.

Statistics
Income from 2000 to 2016 (median income for 3-person household):
- 2000—low income: $26,923; middle income: $78, 056; high income: $183, 680
- 2010—low income: $24, 448; middle income: $74,015; high income: $172,152
- 2016—low income: $25,624; middle income: $78,442; high income: $187,872

   *Demonstrates an income widening gap between low- and middle-income households to high income.

2016 Gallup Poll on Capitalism and Free Enterprise % Positive View
- Americans, all ages: Capitalism—60%; Free Enterprise—85%; Socialism—60%
- Americans, aged 18-29 years: Capitalism—57%; Free Enterprise—78%; Socialism—55%

Organizations to Contact

The editors have compiled the following list of organizations concerned with the issues debated in this book. The descriptions are derived from materials provided by the organizations. All have publications or information available for interested readers. The list was compiled on the date of publication of the present volume; the information provided here may change. Be aware that many organizations take several weeks or longer to respond to inquiries, so allow as much time as possible for the receipt of requested materials.

American Enterprise Institute (AEI)
1789 Massachusetts Avenue NW, Washington DC 20036
Phone: (202) 862-5800
Email: none
Website: www.aei.org/
The AEI is a public policy think tank dedicated to democracy, free enterprise, American strength, and a culture of entrepreneurship. Learn about a wide range of topics including economics, values, capitalism, and the free market.

CATO Institute
1000 Massachusetts Avenue, NW, Washington DC 20001-5403
Phone: (202) 842-0200
Email: use contact page on website
Website: www.cato.org
The CATO Institute is a public policy research organization. It is dedicated to free markets, limited government, peace, and the liberty of individuals. Informational materials include downloadable studies on topics such as: free trade, capitalism, property, justice, liberty, toleration, and peace.

Economic Policy Institute (EPI)
1225 Eye Street NW, Suite 600, Washington DC 20005
Phone: (202) 775-8810

Email: epi@epi.org
Website: www.epi.org
The Economic Policy Institute is a nonprofit, nonpartisan organization. The agency is an authoritative source for information concerning economic issues relating to working Americans.

Federal Trade Commission (FTC)
600 Pennsylvania Avenue, NW, Washington DC 20580
Phone: (202) 326-2222
Website: www.ftc.gov
The Federal Trade Commission is the consumer protection agency of the United States. The FTC also is charged with protecting competition and innovation in America's free market economy. The FTC maintains a media resources library providing information on many topics.

Ford Foundation
320 E. 43rd Street, New York, NY 10017
Phone: (212) 573-5000
Website: www.fordfoundation.org
The Ford Foundation is a nonprofit organization interested in obtaining social justice for people around the world. This agency also focuses its energy on issues of workers' rights and how they intersect with capitalism, economics, and finance.

Institute for New Economic Thinking (INET)
300 Park Avenue South, Floor 5, New York, NY 10010
Website: www.ineteconomics.org
The Institute for New Economic Thinking is an organization dedicated to advancing sound economic ideas. The agency conducts research on current economic issues, maintains a global network of experts, and thoroughly supports and encourages students and other learners.

World Economic Forum
350 Madison Avenue, 11th Floor, New York, NY 10017
Phone: (212) 703-2300

Email: forumusa@weforum.org
Website: www.weforum.org
The World Economic Forum is an international organization working to achieve public-private cooperation on a global scale. By focusing on three key areas—the fourth industrial revolution, global problems, and global security—the agency addresses common global concerns.

World Trade Organization (WTO)
Centre William Rappard, Rue de Lausanne, 154, Case postale, 1211 Geneve 2, Switzerland
Phone: +41 (0) 22 739 51 11
Email: enquiries@wto.org
Website: www.wto.org/index.htm
The World Trade Organization is a forum for economic trade and negotiation between world countries and governments. Students can learn about global economic issues and trade between nations through articles, videos, and publications.

For Further Reading

Books

Burgan, Michael. *American Capitalism*. New York, NY: Children's Press, 2012.

Provides an introduction to the economic system of capitalism. Discusses how capitalism is part of US history, and how it effects society.

Hunter, Nick. *What is Socialism?* New York, NY: Gareth Stevens Publishing, 2014.

Learn about the economic system of socialism. Read about countries that have used socialism and their successes and failures.

Johnson, Martin. *Consumerism*. New York, NY: Mason Crest, 2017.

Analyzes the world of consumerism today and how it affects businesses, culture, young people, and poor countries.

Kaufman, Cynthia. *Getting Past Capitalism: History, Vision, Hope*. Minneapolis, MN: Lexington Books, 2014.

Critique of capitalism and its effects on human society and the environment. Takes a look at the alternative economic systems besides capitalism.

Kenney, Karen Latchana. *What is Communism?* New York, NY: Gareth Stevens Publishing, 2014.

Find out about communism and how it is practiced by countries around the world today, and how it affects people and global politics.

Langone, Kenneth G. *I Love Capitalism!: An American Story*. New York, NY: Portfolio Penguin, 2018.

The founder of Home Depot writes a book showing his belief that capitalism and the free market is a system that works. He details his rise from childhood poverty to success and argues that anyone can live the dream.

Norman, Jesse. *Adam Smith: Father of Economics*. New York, NY: Basic Books, Hachette Books Group, 2018.

Profiles Adam Smith who is considered to be the greatest economist of all time. Gives an understanding of Smith, the time in which he lived, and greater knowledge of the economic principles which he championed.

Reich, Robert B. *Saving Capitalism: For the Many, Not the Few*. New York, NY: Alfred A. Knopf, 2015.

Shows how the economic system of America may be failing. Outlines how a newly designed market may increase broad prosperity instead of limited opportunity.

Periodicals and Internet Sources

Barber, Nigel. "Why Greed Is Bad for Capitalism," Huffpost, October 13, 2010. https://www.huffingtonpost.com/nigel-barber/why-greed-is-bad-for-capi_b_759907.html.

Block, Fred. "To Reform Capitalism, Look to Marx," Institute for New Economic Thinking, May 16, 2018. https://www.ineteconomics.org/perspectives/blog/to-reform-capitalism-look-to-marx.

Cole, Nicki Lisa. "The Globalization of Capitalism," Thought Co., March 18, 2017. https://www.thoughtco.com/globalization-of-capitalism-3026076.

Edwards, Haley. "How Capitalism Lost Its Way," *Washington Monthly*, November/December 2018. https://washingtonmonthly.com/magazine/november-december-2018/how-capitalism-lost-its-way/.

Farmer, Brian. "Capitalism, Socialism, & Christianity," New American, December 30, 2011. https://www.thenewamerican.com/economy/commentary/item/4131-capitalism-socialism—christianity.

Forbes, Steves. "Capitalism: A True Love Story," *Forbes*, October 1, 2009. https://www.forbes.com/forbes/2009/1019/opinions-steve-forbes-capitalism-true-love-story.html#18229e0862de.

Foster, John Bellamy. "Capitalism and Environmental Catastrophe," Resilience, November 5, 2011. https://www.resilience.org/stories/2011-11-05/capitalism-and-environmental-catastrophe/.

Gutting, Gary. "Less, Please," Commonweal, December 26, 2012. https://www.commonwealmagazine.org/less-please.

Lebowitz, Michael A. "What Keeps Capitalism Going?" Monthly Review, June 1, 2004. https://monthlyreview.org/2004/06/01/what-keeps-capitalism-going/.

Magdoff, Fred. "An Ecologically Sound and Socially Just Economy," Monthly Review, September 1, 2014. https://monthlyreview.org/2014/09/01/an-ecologically-sound-and-socially-just-economy/.

Mason, Paul. "Why Marx is More Relevant Than Ever in the Age of Automation," New Statesman America, May 7, 2018. https://www.newstatesman.com/culture/2018/05/why-marx-more-relevant-ever-age-automation.

Ryn, Claes G. "Conservatives in Denial," American Conservative, October 26, 2016. https://www.theamericanconservative.com/articles/conservatives-in-denial/.

Selbourne, David. "How the Left Was Lost: The Need to Relearn What True Progress Means," New Statesman America, July 24, 2014. https://www.newstatesman.com/politics/2014/07/how-left-was-lost-need-relearn-what-true-progress-means.

Thompson, Patricia. "Is There a Place for Compassion in Business?" Garrison Institute, January 4, 2018. https://www.garrisoninstitute.org/blog/is-there-a-place-for-compassion-in-business/.

Tweedy, Rod. "A Mad World: Capitalism and the Rise of Mental Illness," Red Pepper, August 9, 2017. https://www.redpepper.org.uk/a-mad-world-capitalism-and-the-rise-of-mental-illness/.

Zakaria, Fareed. "Zakaria: A Capitalistic Manifesto," Newsweek, June 12, 2009. https://www.newsweek.com/zakaria-capitalist-manifesto-80303.

Websites

American Enterprise Institute (www.aei.org/academic-programs/)
The website of the American Enterprise Institute, AEI, maintains a site geared toward students. Learn about values and capitalism by choosing this link.

Cato Institute (www.cato.org/cato-university/home-study-course)

The Cato Institute website contains a link to a free, downloadable study course where individuals can learn about free trade, capitalism, property, liberty, justice, the US Constitution, government, toleration, and peace.

Economic Policy Institute (www.epi.org/resources/budget/)

The Economic Policy Institute offers a family budget calculator. At this site individuals can work out an estimated monthly budget for different family types (one or two adults with zero to four children) which would pertain to any metro area in the United States.

Institute for Economic Thinking (www.ineteconomics.org/education)

The Institute for Economic Thinking offers courses on money and banking, capitalism, and macroeconomics. Use this link to access the page displaying available courses.

Index

V

Venkatasubramanian,
    Venkat, 56–59
VisionSpring, 98

W

Warby Parker, 98
Wealth of Nations, The, 9,
    23, 35, 93
Whaley, Floyd, 60–68
Whittaker, Martin, 76–81
Williams, Walter, 51–54, 74
*Winner Take All Politics: How
    Washington Made the Rich
    Richer*, 45
Workers World, 69–74
World Economic Forum, 66,
    101–106, 77
World Wildlife Fund, 94, 97

Z

Zipline, 105

Picture Credits